TRAVELMATE

compiled by
LEXUS
with
Galina Androchnikova
and
Sally Davies

Chambers

Published 1992 by W & R Chambers Ltd,
43-45 Annandale Street, Edinburgh EH7 4AZ

**British Library Cataloguing in Publication
Data**

A catalogue record for this book is available from
the British Library.

ISBN 0 550 22004 6

Printed and bound in Great Britain by
Cox & Wyman Ltd.

YOUR TRAVELMATE

gives you one single easy-to-use list of useful
words and phrases to help you communicate in
Russian.

Built into this list are:

– Travel Tips with facts and figures which
  provide valuable information

– typical replies to some of the things you might
  want to say.

And on page 125 you'll find a list of Russian
words that you'll see on signs and notices.

The Russian alphabet is on page 4.

There is a menu reader on pages 68-70. Numbers
are on pages 126-127. On page 128, there's a list
of Republics, cities and places of interest.

Your TRAVELMATE also tells you how to
pronounce Russian. Just read the
pronunciations as though they were English and
you will communicate - although you might not
sound like a native speaker.

Some notes on Russian sounds:

e should be pronounced as in 'wet'
g should be pronounced as in 'get'
H should be pronounced like the 'ch' in Scottish
'loch'
i should be pronounced as in 'bid'
I should be pronounced like the 'y' in 'my'
J should be pronounced like the 's' in 'treasure'
o should always be pronounced as in 'hot' (never
as in 'low')
Vowels in italics show which part of a word to
stress.

In the phrases, *(men/women)* indicates the form
to be used by men and women speakers
respectively.

Your TRAVELMATE gives the pronunciation
before the Russian characters.

THE CYRILLIC ALPHABET

А	а	*A*	a *as in Anne*
Б	б	*BEH*	b
В	в	*VEH*	v
Г	г	*GEH*	g or v
Д	д	*DEH*	d
Е	е	*YEH*	ye *as in yes*
Ё	ё	*YO*	yo *as in yonder*
Ж	ж	*JEH*	s *as in leisure*
З	з	*ZEH*	z *as in zero*
И	и	*EE*	ee
Й	й	*EE KRATKA-YEH*	y *as in toy or silent*
К	к	*KA*	k
Л	л	*EL*	l
М	м	*EM*	m
Н	н	*EN*	n
О	о	*O*	o *as in hot but* a *when unstressed*
П	п	*PEH*	p
Р	р	*ER*	r
С	с	*ES*	s
Т	т	*TEH*	t
У	у	*OO*	oo *as in boot*
Ф	ф	*EF*	f
Х	х	*HA*	ch *as in the Scottish word loch*
Ц	ц	*TSEH*	ts *as in cats*
Ч	ч	*CHEH*	ch *as in chat*
Ш	ш	*SHA*	sh *as in shop*
Щ	щ	*SHA*	sh
Ъ	ъ	*TVYORDI ZNAK*	hard sign – no sound but indicates small pause
Ы	ы	*IY*	i *as in bid*
Ь	ь	*MYAGKEE ZNAK*	soft sign – no sound but softens preceding letter
Э	э	*EH*	e *as in end*
Ю	ю	*YOO*	you *as in youth*
Я	я	*YA*	ya *as in yard*

a, an *there is no word for 'a' in Russian*

abdomen Jeevot [живот]

aboard: aboard the ship/plane na karabl*yeh*/samal*yotyeh* [на корабле/самолёте]

about: is he about? on zdyes? [он здесь?]

   about 15 *o*kala pyatn*a*dsatee [около пафятнадцати]

   about 2 o'clock *o*kala dvooH chas*o*f [около двух часов]

above nad [над]

abroad za gran*ee*tsay [за границей]

accelerator aksyelyer*a*ter [акселератор]

accept preeneem*a*t [принимать]

accident nyesh*a*stni sl*oo*chI [несчастный случай]

   there's been an accident pra-eezash*o*l nyesh*a*stni sl*oo*chI [произошёл несчастный случай]

accommodation Jeel*yo* [жильё]

   we need accommodation for three *(flat)* nam n*oo*Jna kvart*ee*ra na tro-*ee*H [нам нужна квартира на троих]

accurate t*o*chni [точный]

ache: my back aches oo men*ya* bal*ee*t speen*a* [у меня болит спина]

across cher*yez* [через]

   how do we get across? kak pap*a*st na too storan*oo*? [как попасть на ту сторону?]

adaptor ad*a*pter [адаптор]; *see* **electricity**

address *a*dryes [адрес]

» *TRAVEL TIP: a Russian address is usually written in the following order: postcode, republic, region, city/town*
    street, number, flat number
    name

will you give me your address? ast*a*vtyeh
mnyeh vash *a*dryes [оставьте мне ваш адрес]

adjust preespasobeet [приспособить]

admission: how much is the admission?
skolka sto-eet fHot? [сколько стоит вход?]

advance: can we book in advance? mo*J*na
zaka*z*at zar*a*nyeh-yeh? [можно заказать
заранее?]

advert ryekl*a*ma [реклама]

afraid: I'm afraid (of) ya ba-*yoos* [я боюсь]

   I'm afraid so k*a*Jetsa, da [кажется, да]

   I'm afraid not k*a*Jetsa, nyet [кажется, нет]

after: after you p*o*slee vas [после вас]

   after 2 o'clock poslee dvoo*H* chas*o*f [после
   двух часов]

afternoon: in the afternoon dnyom [днём]

   good afternoon d*o*bri dyen [добрый день]

   this afternoon syev*o*dnya dnyom [сегодня
   днём]

aftershave lasy*o*n p*o*slee breet*ya* [лосьон после
бритья]

again snova [снова]

against proteef [против]

age v*o*zrast [возраст]

   under age nyesavyershena-l*y*etnee
   [несовершеннолетний]

   it takes ages *e*ta *o*chen d*o*lga [это очень
   долго]

ago: a week ago nyed*y*elyoo na*z*at [неделю
назад]

   it wasn't long ago *e*ta b*i*yla nyeh tak davno
   [это было не так давно]

   how long ago was that? kak davn*o* *e*ta b*i*yla?
   [как давно это было?]

agree: I agree *(men/women)* ya sagl*a*syen/
sagl*a*sna [я согласен/согласна]

   fish doesn't agree with me ya r*i*yboo nyeh
   yem [я рыбу не ем]

Aids speed [СПИД]

air vo*z*doo*H* [воздух]

   by air samal*y*otam [самолётом]

   by airmail *a*vee-ya p*o*chtoy [авиапочтой]

air-conditioning: with air-conditioning
skandeetsee-onyeram [с кондиционером]
airport eraport [аэропорт]
alarm clock boodeelneek [будильник]
alcohol speertno-yeh [спиртное]
alcoholic: is it alcoholic? eta speertno-yeh?
[это спиртное?]
alive: is he still alive? on yesho Jeev? [он ещё
жив?]
all fsyo [всё]
  all these people fsyeh etee lyoodee [все эти
  люди]
  that's all eta fsyo [это всё]
  that's all wrong fsyo nyeh tak [всё не так]
  all right Harasho [хорошо]
  thank you – not at all spaseeba - nyeh za shto
  [спасибо – не за что]
allergic: I'm allergic to penicillin oo menya
alyergee-ya na pyeneetseeleen [у меня
аллергия на пенициллин]
allow: allow me razresheetyeh mnyeh
[разрешите мне]
  is it allowed? eta moJna? [это можно?]
  that's not allowed eta nyelzya [это нельзя]
almost pachtee [почти]
alone (man/woman) adeen/adna [один/одна]
  leave me alone astavtyeh menya vpako-yeh
  [оставьте меня в покое]
already ooJeh [уже]
also toJeh [тоже]
although Hatya [хотя]
**altogether: what does that make
altogether?** skolka eta vsyevo? [сколько это
всего?]
always fsyegda [всегда]
a.m.: at 8 a.m. v vosem chasof ootra [в восемь
часов утра]
ambassador pasol [посол]
ambulance skora-ya pomosh [скорая помощь]
  get an ambulance! viyzaveetyeh skoroo-yoo
  pomosh! [вызовите скорую помощь!]
» *TRAVEL TIP: to call an ambulance dial 03*

....

America Amyereeka [Америка]
American *(adj)* amyereekanski
  [американский]
among sryedee [среди]
amp: 13-amp fuse predaHraneetyel na
  treenadsat ampyer [предохранитель на
  тринадцать ампер]
anchor yaker [якорь]
and ee [и]
angry syerdeet [сердит]
  I'm very angry about it *(men/women)* ya
  ochen syerdeet/syerdeeta na eta [я очень
  сердит/сердита на это]
  please don't get angry paJalsta, nyeh
  syerdeetyes [пожалуйста, не сердитесь]
animal Jeevotna-yeh [животное]
ankle ladiyshka [лодыжка]
anniversary: it's our anniversary eta nash
  yoobeelyay [это наш юбилей]
annoy: he's annoying me on menya
  razdraJa-yet [он меня раздражает]
  it's very annoying eta ochen razdraJa-yet [это
  очень раздражает]
another: can we have another room? moJna
  droogoy nomyer? [можно другой номер?]
  another beer, please yesho adno peeva,
  paJalsta [ещё одно пиво, пожалуйста]
answer: what was his answer? shto on
  atvyeteel? [что он ответил?]
  there was no answer tam neekto nyeh
  atvyeteel [там никто не ответил]
antique anteekvaree-at [антиквариат]
  » *TRAVEL TIP: export of antiques from Russia is*
  restricted and subject to tax; check the
  regulations before buying
any: have you got any apples/butter? oo vas
  yest yablakee/masla? [у вас есть
  яблоки/масло?]
  I haven't got any oo menya nyet [у меня нет]
anybody kto-neebood [кто-нибудь]
  can anybody help? kto-neebood moJet
  pamoch? [кто-нибудь может помочь?]

anything shto-neebood [что-нибудь]
  I don't want anything mnyeh neechevo nyeh
  Hochetsa [мне ничего не хочется]
aperitif apyereeteef [аперитив]
apology: please accept my apologies
  eezveeneetyeh, paJalsta [извините,
  пожалуйста]
appendicitis apyendeetseet [аппендицит]
appetite apyeteet [аппетит]
  I've lost my appetite (men/women)
  ya patyeryal/patyeryala apyeteet
  [я потерял/потеряла аппетит]
apple yablaka [яблоко]
application form za-yafka [заявка]
appointment: can I make an appointment?
  moJna dagavareetsa a fstryecheh? [можно
  договориться о встрече?]
apricot abreekos [абрикос]
April apryel [апрель]
archaeology arHeh-alogee-ya [археология]
area (neighbourhood) rI-on [район]
  in the area v rI-onyeh [в районе]
arm rooka [рука]
around vakroog [вокруг]
arrange: will you arrange it? viy eta
  oostro-eetyeh? [вы это устроите?]
  it's all arranged fsyo oostro-yena [всё
  устроено]
arrest (verb) aryestavat [арестовать]
  he's been arrested yevo aryestavalee [его
  арестовали]
arrival pree-yezd [приезд]
arrive pree-yeHat [приехать]
  we only arrived yesterday miy tolka fchera
  pree-yeHalee [мы только вчера приехали]
art eeskoostva [искусство]
art gallery karteena-ya galyeryeh-ya
  [картинная галерея]
arthritis artreet [артрит]
artificial eeskoostvyeni [искусственный]
artist HoodoJneek [художник]
as: as quickly as you can kak moJna

· ·

bistr*yeh*-yeh [как можно быстрее]

as much as you can kak mo*J*na bolsheh [как можно больше]

as you like kak *H*ochesh [как хочешь]

ashore na byeryeg*oo* [на берегу]

ashtray p*y*epyelneetsa [пепельница]

ask papras*eet* [попросить]

could you ask him to ...? papras*ee*tyeh yevo, pa*J*alsta ... [попросите его, пожалуйста ...]

that's not what I asked for *(men/women)* eta nyeh to, shto ya papras*eel*/papras*ee*la [это не то, что я попросил/попросила]

asleep: he's still asleep on yesh*o* speet [он ещё спит]

aspirin aspeer*ee*n [аспирин]

assistant asees*t*yent [ассистент]

asthma *a*stma [астма]

at: at the cafe v kaf*eh* [в кафе]

at my hotel oo men*ya* v gast*ee*neetseh [у меня в гостинице]

at one o'clock fchas dnya [в час дня]

atmosphere atmasf*y*era [атмосфера]

attitude atnash*e*nee-yeh [отношение]

attractive preevlyek*a*tyelni [привлекательный]

I think you're very attractive ya d*oo*ma-yoo, viy *o*chen preevlyek*a*tyelni [я думаю, вы очень привлекательны]

aubergine bakla*J*an [баклажан]

August *a*vgoost [август]

aunt t*yo*tya [тётя]

Australia Avstr*a*lee-ya [Австралия]

Australian *(adj)* avstral*ee*skee [австралийский]

authorities vl*a*stee [власти]

automatic aftamat*ee*cheskee [автоматический]

autumn: in the autumn os*e*nyoo [осенью]

away: is it far away from here? *e*ta dalyek*o* atsy*oo*da? [это далеко отсюда?]

go away! ooHad*ee*! [уходи!]

awful oo*J*asni [ужасный]

axle os [ось]
baby ryebyonak [ребёнок]
  we'd like a baby-sitter nam nooJna nyanya [нам нужна няня]
» *TRAVEL TIP: baby-sitters in Moscow are provided by some cooperatives; details can be found on embassy noticeboards*
back: I've got a bad back oo menya balna-ya speena [у меня больная спина]
  I'll be back soon ya skora vyernoos [я скоро вернусь]
  is he back? on vyernoolsa? [он вернулся?]
  can I have my money back? vyerneetyeh mnyeh dyengee [верните мне деньги]
  I go back tomorrow ya oo-yeJa-yoo zaftra [я уезжаю завтра]
  at the back zadee [сзади]
bacon vyetcheena [ветчина]
  bacon and eggs ya-eechneetsa s vyetcheenoy [яичница с ветчиной]
bad ploHa [плохо]
  it's not bad nyeploHa [неплохо]
  too bad! ploHa! [плохо!]
bag soomka [сумка]
baggage bagash [багаж]
baggage claim: where's the baggage claim? gdyeh paloocheet bagaJ? [где получить багаж?]
baker's boolachna-ya [булочная]
balcony balkon [балкон]
  a room with a balcony nomyer sbalkonam [номер с балконом]
ball myach [мяч]
ballet balyet [балет]
ballpoint pen shareekova-ya roochka [шариковая ручка]
banana banan [банан]
band arkyestr [оркестр]
bandage beent [бинт]
  could you change the bandage? pamyenyItyeh beent, paJalsta [поменяйте бинт, пожалуйста]

....

bank bank [банк]

» *TRAVEL TIP: banks in hotels open from 8.45 a.m.
to 8.30 p.m. and close for lunch from 12 to 12.30*

bar bar [бар]

   when does the bar open? kagda atkriva-yetsa
   bar? [когда открывается бар?]

barber's mooJska-ya pareekmaHyerska-ya
[мужская парикмахерская]

bargain: it's a real bargain ochen nyedoraga
[очень недорого]

barmaid barmyensha [барменша]

barman barmyen [бармен]

basket karzeena [корзина]

bath vana [ванна]

   can I have a bath? ya magoo preenyat vanoo?
   [я могу принять ванну?]

   could you give me a bath towel? dJtyeh
   mnyeh, paJalsta, bana-yeh palatyentseh
   [дайте мне, пожалуйста, банное полотенце]

» *TRAVEL TIP: for a Russian-style bathhouse, try
Sandunovsky Bani in Moscow; see* **public bath**

bathing koopanee-yeh [купание]

bathing costume koopalni kastyoom
[купальный костюм]

bathroom vana-ya [ванная]

   we want a room with a private bathroom
   nam nooJen nomyer soodobstvamee [нам
   нужен номер с удобствами]

   can I use your bathroom? moJna
   vaspolzovatsa vasheem too-alyetam? [можно
   воспользоваться вашим туалетом?]

battery bataryayka [батарейка]

» *TRAVEL TIP: take your own supply of batteries*

beach plyaJ [пляж]

beans babiy [бобы]

beautiful kraseevi [красивый]

   that was a beautiful meal miy prekrasna
   pa-yelee [мы прекрасно поели]

because patamoo shto [потому что]

   because of eez-za [из-за]

   because of the weather eez-za pagodi [из-за
   погоды]

bed krav*a*t [кровать]
  single bed/double bed adnasp*a*lna-ya/
  dvoosp*a*lna-ya krav*a*t [односпальная/
  двуспальная кровать]
  you haven't changed my bed viy nyeh
  smyen*ee*lee mnyeh past*y*el [вы не сменили
  мне постель]
  I want to go to bed ya Hach*oo* pl*tee* spat [я
  хочу пойти спать]
  bed and breakfast pansee-on [пансион]
  do you do bed and breakfast? zaftrak
  fkly*oo*chon vst*o*ymast? [завтрак включён в
  стоимость?]
bedroom sp*a*lnya [спальня]
bee pchel*a* [пчела]
beef gav*ya*deena [говядина]
beer p*e*eva [пиво]
  two beers, please dva p*e*eva, paJ*a*lsta [два
  пива, пожалуйста]
» *TRAVEL TIP: beer is usually served in bottles;*
  draught beer is served in large (about a pint)
  and small (about a half-pint) mugs
before: before breakfast pyeryed zaftrakam
  [перед завтраком]
  before we leave pyeryed aty*e*zdam [перед
  отъездом]
  I haven't been here before ya zdyes fpyervi
  raz [я здесь в первый раз]
begin: when does it begin? kagd*a* nach*a*la?
  [когда начало?]
beginner nachee*na*-yooshee [начинающий]
behind za [за]
  the car behind me mash*e*ena za mnoy
  [машина за мной]
believe: I don't believe you ya vam nyeh
  vyery*oo* [я вам не верю]
  I believe you ya vam vyery*oo* [я вам верю]
bell (*in hotel*) zvan*o*k [звонок]
belong: that suitcase belongs to me *e*tat
  chem*a*dan preenadlyeJ*ee*t mnyeh [этот
  чемодан принадлежит мне]
  who does this belong to? chyo *e*ta? [чьё это?]

....

below pod [под]

belt ryemyen [ремень]

bend *(noun: in road)* pavarot [поворот]

berries yagadi [ягоды]

berth *(ship)* koyka [койка]

beside ryadam [рядом]

best loochshee [лучший]

  it's the best holiday I've ever had eta moy sami loochshee otpoosk [это мой самый лучший отпуск]

better loochsheh [лучше]

  haven't you got anything better? oo vas yest shto-neebood paloochsheh? [у вас есть что-нибудь получше?]

  are you feeling better? vam paloochsheh? [вам получше?]

  I'm feeling a lot better mnyeh namnoga loochsheh [мне намного лучше]

between myeJdoo [между]

beyond za [за]

bicycle vyelaseepyet [велосипед]

  can we hire bicycles here? zdyes moJna vzyat naprakat vyelaseepyet? [здесь можно взять напрокат велосипед?]; *see* **cycle**

big balshoy [большой]

  a big one balshoy [большой]

  that's too big sleeshkam balshoy [слишком большой]

  it's not big enough nyedastatachna balshoy [недостаточно большой]

  have you got a bigger one? oo vas yest pabolsheh? [у вас есть побольше?]

bikini beekeenee [бикини]

bill shot [счёт]

  could I have the bill, please? dItyeh mnyeh, paJalsta, shot [дайте мне, пожалуйста, счёт]

bird pteetsa [птица]

birthday dyen raJdyenee-ya [день рождения]

  happy birthday! sdnyom raJdyenee-ya! [с днём рождения!]

  it's my birthday eta moy dyen raJdyenee-ya [это мой день рождения]

biscuit pyech*e*nyeh [печенье]
bit: just a little bit for me mnyeh choot-choot,
 paJ*a*lsta [мне чуть-чуть, пожалуйста]
 that's a bit too expensive *e*ta darogav*a*ta
 [это дороговато]
 a bit of that cake koos*o*chek tav*o* t*o*rta
 [кусочек того торта]
 a big bit balsh*o*y koos*o*k [большой кусок]
bite: I've been bitten *(by dog)* men*y*a
 ookoos*ee*la sab*a*ka [меня укусила собака]
 (by insect) men*y*a pakoos*a*lee nasyek*o*mi-yeh
 [меня покусали насекомые]
bitter *(taste)* g*o*rkee [горький]
black ch*o*rni [чёрный]
 black market ch*o*rni r*i*ynak [чёрный рынок]
 )) *TRAVEL TIP: the black market is widespread:*
 beware of con men, forged banknotes, counterfeit
 foreign and over-priced Russian goods; it's risky
 (and illegal) to change money with people who
 approach you in the street
blackout: he's had a blackout on patyer*ya*l
 saznan*ee*-yeh [он потерял сознание]
bland *(food)* nyeh-*o*stri [неострый]
blanket adyeh-*ya*la [одеяло]
 I'd like another blanket m*o*Jna yesh*o* adn*o*
 adyeh-*ya*la? [можно ещё одно одеяло?]
bleach *(cleaning)* Hl*o*rka [хлорка]
bleed: his nose is bleeding oo n*ye*vo eed*yo*t
 krov eez n*o*sa [у него идёт кровь из носа]
bless you! b*oo*dtyeh zdar*o*vi! [будьте здоровы!]
blind *(cannot see)* slyep*o*y [слепой]
blister: I've got a blister on my finger oo
 men*y*a vald*i*yr na p*a*ltseh [у меня волдырь на
 пальце]
blonde *(noun)* bland*ee*nka [блондинка]
blood krov [кровь]
 his blood group is ... oo n*ye*vo ... gr*oo*pa
 krov*ee* [у него ... группа крови]
 )) *TRAVEL TIP: blood groups*

UK	O	A	B	AB
Russia	*1*	*2*	*3*	*4*

 I've got high blood pressure oo men*y*a

....

visoka-yeh davlyenee-yeh [у меня высокое давление]

Bloody Mary kravava-ya Meree [кровавая Мери]

blouse bloozka [блузка]

blue seenee [синий]

blusher roomyana [румяна]

board: full board polni pansee-on [полный пансион]

》 *TRAVEL TIP: although full board is included with package tours you won't find full-board or half-board rates in Russian hotels as they operate on a 'pay-as-you-eat' basis*

boarding pass pasadachni talon [посадочный талон]

boat lodka [лодка]

 when is the next boat to ...? kagda slyedoo-yooshee ryays v ...? [когда следующий рейс в ...?]

body tyela [тело]

boil *(noun)* nariyv [нарыв]

 (verb) keepyateet [кипятить]

 do we have to boil the water? nooJna keepyateet vodoo? [нужно кипятить воду?]

 boiled egg varyona-yeh yItso [варёное яйцо]

bone kost [кость]

bonnet *(car)* kapot [капот]

book *(noun)* kneega [книга]

can I book a seat for ...? moJna koopeet beelyet na ...? [можно купить билет на ...?]

》 *TRAVEL TIP: for long-distance travel, seats and berths are usually numbered, and you get your seat or berth number when you buy a ticket*

booking office beelyetna-ya kasa [билетная касса]

bookshop kneeJni magazeen [книжный магазин]

》 *TRAVEL TIP: 31 Kropotskinskaya in Moscow has a good selection of foreign language books for hard currency as do 'Dom Kneegee' bookshops in Moscow and St Petersburg*

boot *(shoe)* sapok [сапог]

(of car) bagaJneek [багажник]

booze viypeefka [выпивка]

   I had too much booze last night
(men/women) ya sleeshkam mnoga
viypeel/viypeela fchera [я слишком много
выпил/выпила вчера]

border graneetsa [граница]

bored: I'm bored mnyeh skooshna [мне
скучно]

boring skooshni [скучный]

born: I was born in … *(men/women)* ya
radeelsa/radeelas v … [я родился/родилась
в …]

borrow: can I borrow …? moJna vzyat na
vryemya … [можно взять на время …]

boss boss [босс]

both oba [оба]

   I'll take both of them ya vazmoo oba [я
возьму оба]

bottle bootiylka [бутылка]

bottle-opener atkrivalka [открывалка]

bottom: at the bottom of the hill oo
padnoJee-ya gariy [у подножия горы]

bouncer visheebala [вышибала]

bowels keeshechneek [кишечник]

bowl *(noun)* chashka [чашка]

box karopka [коробка]

boy malcheek [мальчик]

boyfriend drook [друг]

bra byoostgaltyer [бюстгальтер]

bracelet braslyet [браслет]

brake: I had to brake suddenly mnyeh
preeshlos ryezka zatarmazeet [мне пришлось
резко затормозить]

   brakes tarmaza [тормоза]

   could you check the brakes? pravyertyeh
tarmaza, paJalsta [проверьте тормоза,
пожалуйста]

brandy kanyak [коньяк]

bread Hlyeb [хлеб]

   could we have some bread and butter?
dItyeh, paJalsta, Hlyeb smaslam [дайте,

···

пожалуйста, хлеб с маслом]
some more bread, please yesho Hlyeba,
paJalsta [ещё хлеба, пожалуйста]
break *(verb)* slamat [сломать]
  I think I've broken my arm *(men/women)*
  kaJetsa, ya slamal/slamala rookoo [кажется, я
  сломал/сломала руку]
  you've broken it viy yevo slamalee [вы его
  сломали]
  my room/car has been broken into ma-yoo
  komnatoo/masheenoo vzlamalee [мою
  комнату/машину взломали]
breakable Hroopkee [хрупкий]
breakdown: I've had a breakdown oo menya
  slamalas masheena [у меня сломалась
  машина]
  nervous breakdown nyervni sriyv [нервный
  срыв]
breakfast zaftrak [завтрак]
breast grood [грудь]
breath diHanee-yeh [дыхание]
  he's getting very short of breath on
  zadiHa-yetsa [он задыхается]
breathe dishat [дышать]
  I can't breathe ya zadiHa-yoos [я задыхаюсь]
bribe vzyatka [взятка]; *see* tip
bridge most [мост]
briefcase partfyel [портфель]
brilliant *(person, idea)* blyestyashee
  [блестящий]
bring preenyestee [принести]
  could you bring it to my hotel? viy moJetyeh
  preenyestee eta mnyeh v gasteeneetsoo? [вы
  можете принести это мне в гостиницу?]
Britain Vyeleeka-breetanee-ya
  [Великобритания]
British *(adj)* breetanskee [британский]
brochure brashoora [брошюра]
  have you got any brochures about ...? oo
  vas yest brashoori o ...? [у вас есть брошюры
  о ...?]
broken sloman [сломан]

it's broken on sloman [он сломан]
brooch broshka [брошка]
brother brat [брат]
brown kareechnyevi [коричневый]
brown paper abyortachna-ya boomaga
[обёрточная бумага]
bruise *(noun)* seenyak [синяк]
brunette *(noun)* bryoonyetka [брюнетка]
brush *(noun)* shotka [щётка]
bucket vyedro [ведро]
buffet *(on train etc)* boofyet [буфет]
(in restaurant) shvedskee stol [шведский стол]
building zdanee-yeh [здание]
bulb *(electric)* lampachka [лампочка]
the bulb's gone lampachka pyeryegaryela
[лампочка перегорела]
Bulgaria Bolgaree-ya [Болгария]
bump: he's had a bump on the head on
oosheep golavoo [он ушиб голову]
bumper bampyer [бампер]
bunch of flowers bookyet tsvyetof [букет
цветов]
bunk koyka [койка]
burglar vor [вор]
YOU MAY WANT TO SAY …
they've taken all my money oo menya
ookralee fsyeh dyengee [у меня украли все
деньги]
**burn: can you give me something for these
burns?** oo vas yest shto-neebood at aJogaf? [у
вас есть что-нибудь от ожогов?]
this meat is burnt myasa padgaryela [мясо
подгорело]
my arms are burnt *(sunburnt)* oo menya
abgaryelee rookee [у меня обгорели руки]
bus aftoboos [автобус]
bus stop aftoboosna-ya astanofka [автобусная
остановка]
YOU MAY WANT TO ASK …
could you tell me when we get there? viy
mnyeh skaJetyeh, gdyeh viHadeet? [вы мне
скажете, где выходить?]

....

>> *TRAVEL TIP: long-distance bus travel is more uncomfortable and much slower than the train and is not recommended*

business: I'm here on business ya zdyes v kamandeerovkyeh [я здесь в командировке]

business trip kamandeerovka [командировка]

none of your business! nyeh vasheh dyela! [не ваше дело!]

bust byoost [бюст]

busy zanyata [занято]

are you busy? viy zanyati? [вы заняты?]

but no [но]

not this one but that one nyeh tot, a etat [не тот, а этот]

butcher's myasnoy magazeen [мясной магазин]

butter masla [масло]

button poogaveetsa [пуговица]

buy: I'll buy it ya eta pakoopa-yoo [я это покупаю]

where can I buy ...? gdyeh moJna koopeet ...? [где можно купить ...?]

by: I'm here by myself *(men/women)* ya zdyes adeen/adna [я здесь один/одна]

are you by yourself? *(to a man/woman)* tiy adeen/adna? [ты один/одна?]

can you do it by tomorrow? viy moJetyeh zdyelat eta k zaftrashnyemoo dnyoo? [вы можете сделать это к завтрашнему дню?]

by train/by car/by plane po-yezdam/masheenoy/samalyotam [поездом/машиной/самолётом]

cabaret kabaray [кабаре]

cabbage kapoosta [капуста]

cabin *(on ship)* ka-yoota [каюта]

cable *(electric)* kabyel [кабель]

cable car fooneekyoolyor [фуникулёр]

café kafeh [кафе]

cake tort [торт]

a piece of cake koosok torta [кусок торта]

calculator kalkoolyater [калькулятор]

call pazv*a*t [позвать]
  will you call the manager? pazav*ee*tyeh admeeneestr*a*tera [позовите администратора]
  what is this called? kak *e*ta naziv*a*-yetsa? [как это называется?]
call box tyelyef*o*n-aftam*a*t [телефон-автомат]
calm *(sea)* spak*o*yni [спокойный]
  calm down! oospak*o*ytyes! [успокойтесь!]
camcorder veedeh-ohk*a*myera [видеокамера]
camera f*o*to-apar*a*t [фотоаппарат]
camping gas g*a*zavi bal*o*ncheek [газовый баллончик]
can[1]: **a can of beer** b*a*nka p*ee*va [банка пива]
can[2]: **can I have ...?** d*I*tyeh mnyeh, paJ*a*lsta ... [дайте мне, пожалуйста ...]
  can you show me ...? pakaJ*ee*tyeh, paJ*a*lsta ... [покажите, пожалуйста ...]
  I can't ... ya nyeh mag*oo* ... [я не могу ...]
  he can't ... on nyeh m*o*Jet ... [он не может ...]
  we can't ... miy nyeh m*o*Jem ... [мы не можем ...]
Canada Kan*a*da [Канада]
Canadian *(adj)* kan*a*dskee [канадский]
cancel: I want to cancel my booking ya Hach*oo* atmyen*ee*t zak*a*s [я хочу отменить заказ]
  can we cancel dinner for tonight? m*o*Jna atmyen*ee*t oo*J*een na syev*o*dnya? [можно отменить ужин на сегодня?]
candle svyech*a* [свеча]
can-opener atkriv*a*lka [открывалка]
capitalism kapeetal*ee*zm [капитализм]
capsize: the boat's capsized l*o*dka oprak*ee*noolas [лодка опрокинулась]
car mash*ee*na [машина]
  by car na mash*ee*nyeh [на машине]
carafe graf*ee*n [графин]
carburettor karbyoor*a*ter [карбюратор]
card *(business)* veez*ee*tka [визитка]
cards k*a*rti [карты]
  do you play cards? viy eegr*a*-yetyeh v k*a*rti?

....

[вы играете в карты?]

care: goodbye, take care dasveedanee-ya,
fsyevo Haroshyeva [до свидания, всего
хорошего]

will you take care of this suitcase for me?
preesmatreetyeh za ma-eem chemadanam,
paJalsta [присмотрите за моим чемоданом,
пожалуйста]

careful: be careful boodtyeh astaroJni [будьте
осторожны]

carp karp [карп]

car park sta-yanka [стоянка]

carpet kavyor [ковёр]

carrot markof [морковь]

carry: will you carry this for me?
panyeseetyeh eta, paJalsta [понесите это,
пожалуйста]

carving ryezba [резьба]

case (*suitcase*) chemadan [чемодан]

cash naleechni-yeh dyengee [наличные деньги]

I haven't any cash oo menya nyet pree sebyeh
naleechniH dyenyeg [у меня нет при себе
наличных денег]

will you cash a cheque for me? moJna lee
zdyes pamyenyat chek na naleechni-yeh?
[можно ли здесь поменять чек на
наличные?]

cash desk kasa [касса]

cassette kasyeta [кассета]

cassette recorder kasyetneek [кассетник]

cat koshka [кошка]

catch: where do we catch the bus? gdyeh miy
moJem syest na aftoboos? [где мы можем
сесть на автобус?]

he's caught a bug on preebalyel [он
приболел]

cathedral sabor [собор]

Catholic (*adj*) kataleecheskee [католический]

cauliflower tsvyetna-ya kapoosta [цветная
капуста]

cave pyeshera [пещера]

caviar eekra [икра]

ceiling patalok [потолок]

celery syeldyer*ya*y [сельдерей]

centigrade pa Tselsee-yoo [по Цельсию]

» *TRAVEL TIP: to convert C to F:* $\frac{C}{5} \times 9 + 32 = F$

centigrade	-15	-5	0	10	15	21	36.9
Fahrenheit	5	23	32	50	59	70	98.4

centimetre santeemy*e*tr [сантиметр]

» *TRAVEL TIP: 1 cm = 0.39 inches*

central tsentr*a*lni [центральный]

central heating tsentr*a*lna-yeh atapl*y*enee-yeh [центральное отопление]

» *TRAVEL TIP: central heating is installed everywhere; wear layers of clothing that can be easily removed as it's often too hot inside*

centre tsentr [центр]

  how do we get to the city centre? kak pap*a*st vtsentr gor*a*da? [как попасть в центр города?]

certain oovy*e*ryen [уверен]

  are you certain? viy oovy*e*ryeni? [вы уверены?]

chain tsep [цепь]

  (necklace) tsep*o*chka [цепочка]

chair stool [стул]

chambermaid gorn*ee*chna-*ya* [горничная]

champagne shamp*a*nska-yeh [шампанское]

change: could you change this into roubles? viy m*o*Jetyeh pamy*e*nyat eta na roobl*ee*? [вы можете поменять это на рубли?]

  I haven't any change oo men*ya* nyet my*e*lachee [у меня нет мелочи]

  do we have to change trains? nam n*oo*Jna d*y*elat pyeryes*a*tkoo? [нам нужно делать пересадку?]

  I'll just get changed sy*a*ychas viy pyery*e*yeh-ady*e*noos [сейчас я переоденусь]

charge: what will you charge? sk*o*lka viy za *e*ta vazm*yo*tyeh? [сколько вы за это возьмёте?]

  who's in charge? kto za *e*ta atvyech*a*-yet? [кто за это отвечает?]

....

chart sHyema [схема]
cheap dyosheva [дёшево]
  have you got something cheaper? oo vas
  nyet neechevo padyeshevlyeh? [у вас нет
  ничего подешевле?]
cheat: I've been cheated menya abmanoolee
  [меня обманули]
check: will you check? viy pravyereetyeh? [вы
  проверите?]
  I'm sure, I've checked ya tochna pravyereel
  [я точно проверил]
  will you check the total? pravyertyeh
  soomoo, paJalsta [проверьте сумму,
  пожалуйста]
cheek sheka [щека]
cheeky nagli [наглый]
cheerio paka [пока]
cheers! *(toast)* vasheh zdarovyeh! [ваше
  здоровье!]
  (thank you) blagadaryoo! [благодарю!]
cheese siyr [сыр]
  say cheese! oolibneetyes! [улыбнитесь!]
chef shef [шеф]
chemist's aptyeka [аптека]
》 *TRAVEL TIP: medicines are difficult to find,*
  especially those for colds, and will almost
  certainly have a different brand name; take any
  medicines you might need with you
cheque chek [чек]
  will you take a cheque? moJna aplateet
  chekam? [можно оплатить чеком?]
》 *TRAVEL TIP: in most places outwith the black*
  market where you can use hard currency you'll
  be able to pay by traveller's cheque or credit card
  (supported by an ID), although cash is usually
  preferred; see also **traveller's cheque**
chest grood [грудь]
chewing gum Jvachka [жвачка]
chickenpox vyetryanka [ветрянка]
child ryebyonak [ребёнок]
  children dyetee [дети]
  children's portion dyetska-ya portsee-ya

[детская порция]

chin padbarodak [подбородок]

china farfor [фарфор]

China KeetI [Китай]

Chinese *(adj)* keetIskee [китайский]

chips cheepsi [чипсы]

chocolate shakalad [шоколад]

  hot chocolate garyachee shakalad [горячий шоколад]

  a box of chocolates karopka shakaladniH kanfyet [коробка шоколадных конфет]

choke *(car)* startyor [стартёр]

chop *(noun)* atbeevna-ya [отбивная]

  pork/lamb chop sveena-ya/baranya atbeevna-ya [свиная/баранья отбивная]

Christian name eemya [имя]

Christmas RaJdyestvo [Рождество]

» *TRAVEL TIP: Orthodox Christmas (January 7) is an official holiday in Russia but 25-26 December is not*

church tserkaf [церковь]

  where is the Orthodox/Protestant/ Catholic Church? gdyeh pravaslavna-ya/ pratestanstka-ya/katale echeska-ya tserkaf? [где православная/протестантская/ католическая церковь?]

cigar seegara [сигара]

cigarette seegaryeta [сигарета]

  (Russian, non-filter) papirosa [папироса]

  would you like a cigarette? Hateetyeh seegaryetoo? [хотите сигарету?]

cinema keeno [кино]

» *TRAVEL TIP: foreign films are usually dubbed into Russian*

circle kroog [круг]

  (in cinema) balkon [балкон]

city gorat [город]

claim *(insurance)* tryebavanee-yeh a viplatyeh straHofkee [требование о выплате страховки]

clarify ootachneet [уточнить]

clean *(adj)* cheesti [чистый]

can I have some clean sheets?
pamyenya-yetyeh mnyeh belyo, paJalsta
[поменяйте мне бельё, пожалуйста]

my room hasn't been cleaned today ma-yoo
komnatoo syevodnya nyeh oobralee [мою
комнату сегодня не убрали]

it's not clean eta gryazna-yeh [это грязное]

cleaning solution *(contact lens)* rastvor dlya
leenz [раствор для линз]

cleansing cream acheesha-yooshee kryem
[очищающий крем]

clear: I'm not clear about it mnyeh nyeh
savsyem panyatna [мне не совсем понятно]

clever oomni [умный]

climate kleemat [климат]

» *TRAVEL TIP: in Moscow the hottest months are
July and August and the coldest period is from
November to the middle of April; St Petersburg
has a lot of rain; the climate in Southern Russia
is sub-tropical*

cloakroom *(for coats)* gardyerop [гардероб]

» *TRAVEL TIP: you may be asked to leave your
overcoats in the cloakroom even in a very small
café; you'll be given coat tags in most places
(WC)* too-alyet [туалет]; *see* **toilet**

clock chasiy [часы]

close[1] *(nearby)* nyedalyeko [недалеко]
(weather) dooshni [душный]

close[2]**: when do you close?** kagda viy
zakriva-yetyeh? [когда вы закрываете?]

closed zakriyta [закрыто]

cloth tkan [ткань]
(rag) tryapka [тряпка]

clothes adyeJda [одежда]

cloud oblaka [облако]

clutch stseplyenee-yeh [сцепление]

coach myeJdoo-garodni aftoboos
[междугородный автобус]

coach party toorgroopa [тургруппа]

coast byeryek [берег]

coastguard byeryegava-ya aHrana [береговая
охрана]

coat palto [пальто]

cockroach tarakan [таракан]

》 *TRAVEL TIP: you might find them in your hotel room; spray your room and especially the bathroom with insect repellent when you arrive*

coffee kofeh [кофе]

a coffee, please chashkoo kofeh, paJalsta [чашку кофе, пожалуйста]

》 *TRAVEL TIP: in restaurants, coffee is usually served strong, black and already sweetened; milk is not supplied and you'll have to ask for it; in fast food places, coffee is served weak with a lot of milk and sugar*

coin manyeta [монета]

cold *(adj)* Halodni [холодный]

I'm cold mnyeh Holadna [мне холодно]

I've got a cold oo menya prastooda [у меня простуда]

collapse: he's collapsed on patyeryal saznanee-yeh [он потерял сознание]

collar varatneek [воротник]

collect: I want to collect … *(men/women)* ya preeshol/preeshla za … [я пришёл/пришла за …]

colour tsvyet [цвет]

have you any other colours? yest droogee-yeh tsvyeta? [есть другие цвета?]

comb rashoska [расчёска]

come preeHadeet [приходить]

I come from London ya eez Londana [я из Лондона]

we came here yesterday miy pree-yeHalee fchera [мы приехали вчера]

come on! davI skaryay! [давай скорей!]

come here eedeetyeh syooda [идите сюда]

comfortable oodobni [удобный]

it's not very comfortable nyeh ochen oodobna [не очень удобно]

communism kamooneezm [коммунизм]

communist *(noun)* kamooneest [коммунист] *(adj)* kamooneesteecheskee [коммунистический]

Communist party kamooneesteecheska-ya partee-ya [коммунистическая партия]

compact disk kampakt-deesk [компакт-диск]

company *(business)* feerma [фирма]
  you're good company svamee pree-yatna pravadeet vryemya [с вами приятно проводить время]

compartment *(train)* koopeh [купе]

compass kompas [компас]

compensation kampyensatsee-ya [компенсация]

complain Jalavatsa [жаловаться]
  I want to complain about my room/the service *(men/women)*
ya nyedavolyen/nyedavolna sva-eem nomyeram/abslooJeevanee-yem [я недоволен/недовольна своим номером/обслуживанием]

completely savyershena [совершенно]

complicated: it's very complicated ochen sloJna [очень сложно]

compliment: my compliments to the chef skaJeetyeh balsho-yeh spaseeba shef-povaroo [скажите большое спасибо шеф-повару]

computer kampyootyer [компьютер]

concert kantsert [концерт]

concussion satryasyenee-yeh mozga [сотрясение мозга]

condition sasta-yanee-yeh [состояние]
  it's not in very good condition eta nyeh vochen Haroshem sasta-yanee [это не в очень хорошем состоянии]

conditioner kandeetsee-onyer [кондиционер]

condom pryezyervateev [презерватив]; *see* **contraceptive**

conference kanfyeryentsee-ya [конференция]

confirm: I want to confirm … ya Hachoo padtverdeet … [я хочу подтвердить …]

confuse: you're confusing me viy menya zapootalee [вы меня запутали]

congratulations! pazdravlya-yoo! [поздравляю!]

conjunctivitis kanyoonkteeve*et*
[конъюнктивит]

con man mashene*ek* [мошенник]

connection *(travel)* pyerye*sat*ka [пересадка]

connoisseur zna*tok* [знаток]

conscious: he is conscious on v sazn*a*nee [он в
сознании]

consciousness: he's lost consciousness on
paty*er*yal sazn*a*nee-yeh [он потерял
сознание]

constipation za*por* [запор]

consul kon*sool* [консул]

consulate kon*sool*stva [консульство]

contact: how can I contact ...? kak m*oJ*na
svya*zat*sa s ...? [как можно связаться с ...?]

contact lenses kan*tak*tni-yeh l*e*enzi
[контактные линзы]

contraceptive prateevaza*cha*tachna-yeh
s*ryed*stva [противозачаточное средство]

» *TRAVEL TIP: contraceptives are difficult to*
obtain and are of inferior quality; take your own
supply or try hard-currency shops

convenient ood*ob*ni [удобный]

cook *(noun)* *po*var [повар]

it's beautifully cooked zamye*cha*tyelna
pree*ga*tovlyena [замечательно
приготовлено]

cooker *plee*ta [плита]

cool praHl*a*dni [прохладный]

corkscrew sht*o*per [штопор]

corn *(foot)* m*a*zol [мозоль]

corner *(of street, room)* *oo*gol [угол]

can we have a corner table? m*oJ*na za*nyat*
stol voo*gloo*? [можно занять стол в углу?]

cornflakes kookoor*ooz*ni-yeh Hl*o*pya
[кукурузные хлопья]

correct pra*veel*ni [правильный]

cosmetics kasm*ye*teeka [косметика]

cost: what does it cost? sk*ol*ka st*o*-yeet?
[сколько стоит?]

YOU MAY WANT TO SAY ...

that's too much mnoga*va*ta [многовато]

I'll take it ya vazmoo eta [я возьму это]

cotton wool vata [вата]

couchette spalna-yeh myesta [спальное место]

cough *(noun)* kashel [кашель]

cough syrup meekstoora at kashlya [микстура от кашля]

could: could you please …? viy nyeh maglee biy …? [вы не могли бы ..?]

  could I have …? moJna …? [можно ...?]

country *(nation)* strana [страна]

  in the country za goradam [за городом]

couple: a couple of … nyeskolka … [несколько …]

courier rookavadeetyel groopi [руководитель группы]

course: of course kanyeshna [конечно]

cousin *(male/female)* koozyen/koozeena [кузен/кузина]

cover: keep him covered up dyerJeetyeh yevo vteplyeh [держите его в тепле]

cover charge plata za abslooJeevanee-yeh [плата за обслуживание]

cow karova [корова]

crab krab [краб]

crash: there's been a crash pra-eezashla avaree-ya [произошла авария]

crash helmet zasheetni shlem [защитный шлем]

crazy soomashedshee [сумашедший]

  you're crazy! viy sooma sashlee! [вы с ума сошли!]

cream *(on milk)* sleefkee [сливки]
  (in cake, for face) kryem [крем]

creche yaslee [ясли]

credit card kryedeetna-ya kartachka [кредитная карточка]

» *TRAVEL TIP: only of use in big department stores, hotels and restaurants; you must have some form of ID with you*

crisis kreezis [кризис]

crisps cheepsi [чипсы]

crossroads pyeryekryostak [перекрёсток]

crowd talpa [толпа]

cruise kroo-eez [круиз]

crutches (for invalid) kastilee [костыли]

cry: don't cry nyeh plach [не плачь]

culture kooltoora [культура]

cup (china) chashka [чашка]

(plastic) stakan [стакан]

cupboard shkaf [шкаф]

curtains zanavyeskee [занавески]

cushion padooshka [подушка]

Customs tamoJnya [таможня]

» *TRAVEL TIP: customs regulations are worth looking into before you go; on entering and leaving the country, you will be asked to fill out a simple customs form in English*

cut: I've cut my hand (men/women) ya paryezal/paryezala rookoo [я порезал/порезала руку]

cycle: can we cycle there? na vyelaseepyedyeh tooda moJna da-yeHat? [на велосипеде туда можно доехать?]

» *TRAVEL TIP: cycling is popular but dangerous because of dangerous drivers, uneven roads and absence of cycle lanes; cycle thefts are common*

cyclist vyelaseepyedeest [велосипедист]

cylinder tseeleendr [цилиндр]

Czechoslovakia CheHaslavakee-ya [Чехословакия]

dad(dy) papa [папа]

damage: I'll pay for the damage ya zaplachoo za oosherp [я заплачу за ущерб]

damaged pavryeJdyeno [повреждено]

damn! kchortoo! [к чёрту!]

damp siroy [сырой]

dance tanyets [танец]

would you like to dance? moJna preeglaseet vas na tanyets? [можно пригласить вас на танец?]

dangerous apasni [опасный]

dark tyomni [тёмный]

when does it get dark? kagda tyemnyeh-yet? [когда темнеет?]

....

dark blue tyomna-seenee [тёмно-синий]

darling (*male/female*) daragoy/daraga-ya [дорогой/дорогая]

dashboard preeborni sheetok [приборный щиток]

date: what's the date? kako-yeh syevodnya cheeslo? [какое сегодня число?]

can we have a date? (*romantic*) moJna preeglaseet vas na sveedanee-yeh? [можно пригласить вас на свидание?]

can we fix a date? (*business*) moJem dagavareetsa a fstryecheh? [можем договориться о встрече?]

on the fifth of May pyatava ma-ya [пятого мая]

in 1951 v tisyacha dyevyatsot peedeesyat pyervam gadoo [в тысяча девятьсот пятьдесят первом году]

dates (*fruit*) feeneekee [финики]

daughter doch [дочь]

day dyen [день]

have a good day! fsyevo Harosheva! [всего хорошего!]

dazzle: his lights were dazzling me menya aslyepeel svyet far [меня ослепил свет фар]

dead myortvi [мёртвый]

deaf glooHoy [глухой]

deal: it's a deal (*men/women*) saglasyen/saglasna [согласен/согласна]

will you deal with it? viy zImyotyes eteem? [вы займётесь этим?]

dear (*expensive*) daragoy [дорогой]

December dyekabr [декабрь]

deck palooba [палуба]

deckchair shezlong [шезлонг]

deep gloobokee [глубокий]

is it deep? zdyes glooboko? [здесь глубоко?]

delay: the flight was delayed ryays apazdal [рейс опоздал]

deliberately namyerenna [намеренно]

delicate Hroopkee [хрупкий]

delicious fkoosni [вкусный]

it's delicious *e*ta fk*oo*sna [это вкусно]

that was delicious b*y*la ochen fk*oo*sna [было
очень вкусно]

delivery: is there another mail delivery?
b*oo*dyet yesho dast*a*fka pochti? [будет ещё
доставка почты?]

de luxe v*i*ys-shay katyeg*o*ree [высшей
категории]

democratic dyemakrat*ee*cheskee
[демократический]

dent *(noun)* vmyat*ee*na [вмятина]

you've dented my car viy pam*ya*lee ma-*yoo*
mash*ee*noo [вы помяли мою машину]

dentist zoobn*o*y vrach [зубной врач]

YOU MAY HEAR ...

atkro-*ee*tyeh rot! *open wide!*

nyeh zakriv*I*tyeh *keep it open*

sy*a*ychas b*oo*dyet bolna *it's going to hurt now*

dentures zoobn*o*y prat*ye*s [зубной протез]

deodorant dyezadar*a*nt [дезодорант]

departure at*ye*zd [отъезд]

departure lounge zal aJeed*a*nee-ya [зал
ожидания]

depend: it depends on ... *e*ta zav*ee*seet at ...
[это зависит от ...]

deposit zad*a*tak [задаток]

do I have to leave a deposit? n*oo*Jna ast*a*veet
zad*a*tak? [нужно оставить задаток?]

depressed pad*a*vlyeni [подавленный]

depth gloob*ee*n*a* [глубина]

desperate: I'm desperate for a drink ya ochen
Hach*oo* peet [я очень хочу пить]

dessert dyes*ye*rt [десерт]

detergent mo-y*oo*sheh-yeh sry*e*dstva [моющее
средство]

detour: we have to make a detour via ...
n*oo*Jna sd*ye*lat ab*ye*zd cher*ye*z ... [нужно
сделать объезд через ...]

develop: could you develop these? mo*Je*tyeh
pra-yav*ee*t *e*tee plyonkee? [можете проявить
эти плёнки?]

diabetic dee-ab*ye*teek [диабетик]

dialling code kod gorada [код города]
» *TRAVEL TIP: inside the country, Moscow's code
  is 095 and St Petersburg's 812*
diamond breelee-ant [бриллиант]
diarrhoea panos [понос]
  have you got something for diarrhoea?
  oo vas yest shto-neebood at panosa? [у вас
  есть что-нибудь от поноса?]
diary dnyevneek [дневник]
  (business) dyelavoy dnyevneek [деловой
  дневник]
dictionary slavar [словарь]
didn't *see* **not**
die oomeerat [умирать]
  he's dying on oomeera-yet [он умирает]
diesel *(fuel)* deezyelna-yeh topleeva [дизельное
  топливо]
diet dee-yeta [диета]
  I'm on a diet ya na dee-yetyeh [я на диете]
different: they are different anee razni-yeh
  [они разные]
  can I have a different room? moJna
  paloocheet droogoy nomyer? [можно получить
  другой номер?]
  is there a different route? yest drooga-ya
  daroga? [есть другая дорога?]
difficult troodni [трудный]
digestion peesheh-varyenee-yeh [пищеварение]
dining room stalova-ya [столовая]
dinner ooJeen [ужин]
  (midday) abyet [обед]
dinner jacket smoking [смокинг]
direct *(adj)* pryamoy [прямой]
  does this train go direct? eta pryamoy
  po-yezd? [это прямой поезд?]
dirty gryazni [грязный]
disabled *(person)* invaleet [инвалид]
disappear eeschezat [исчезать]
  it's just disappeared prosta eeschez [просто
  исчез]
disappointing: the match was disappointing
  match biyl tak syebyeh [матч был так себе]

disco deeskat*ye*ka [дискотека]
  see you in the disco da fstr*ye*chee v
  deeskat*ye*kyeh [до встречи в дискотеке]
discount skeetka [скидка]
disgusting atvrat*ee*tyelni [отвратительный]
dish bl*yoo*da [блюдо]
dishonest nyech*e*stni [нечестный]
disinfectant dyezeen-feets*ee*roo-yoosheh-yeh
  sr*ye*dstva [дезинфицирующее средство]
dispensing chemist's apt*ye*ka [аптека]
distance rasta-*ya*nee-yeh [расстояние]
distress signal seegn*a*l byedstvee-*ya* [сигнал
  бедствия]
distributor *(car)* raspr*ye*d-yel*ee*tyel
  zaJeeg*a*nee-*ya* [распределитель зажигания]
disturb: the noise is disturbing us nam
  mesha-yet shoom [нам мешает шум]
divorced razvyedyoni [разведённый]
do: how do you do? zdr*a*stvootyeh!
  [здравствуйте!]
  what are you doing tonight? shto viy
  d*ye*la-yetyeh syev*o*dnya v*ye*cheram? [что вы
  делаете сегодня вечером?]
  how do you do it? kak *e*ta d*ye*la-yetsa? [как
  это делается?]
  will you do it for me? paJ*a*lsta, zd*ye*ltyeh *e*ta
  dlya men*ya* [пожалуйста, сделайте это для
  меня]
  I've never done it before ya *e*ta d*ye*la-yoo
  fp*ye*rvi raz [я это делаю в первый раз]
  I was doing 60 (kph) *(men/women)* ya
  *ye*Hal/*ye*Hala sa skorast*yoo* shesdyes*ya*t
  keelam*ye*traf fchas [я ехал/ехала со
  скоростью шестьдесят километров в час]
doctor vrach [врач]
  (as form of address) dokter [доктор]
  I need a doctor mnyeh n*oo*Jen vrach [мне
  нужен врач]
» *TRAVEL TIP: take out medical insurance before
  leaving the UK; you'll have to go to your hotel
  doctor or a clinic for foreigners and will be
  charged*

....

YOU MAY HEAR ...
eta oo vas vpyervi-yeh? *have you had this before?*
gdyeh baleet? *where does it hurt?*
kakee-yeh lyekarstva preeneema-yetyeh? *what medicines are you taking at present?*

document dakoomyent [документ]

dog sabaka [собака]

don't! pyeryestan! [перестань!]; *see also* **not**

door dvyer [дверь]
 (of car) dvyertsa [дверца]

dosage doza [доза]

double room nomyer na dvo-eeH [номер на двоих]

down: it's further down the road eta vpyeryedee [это впереди]
 get down (from) spoosteetsa [спуститься]

downstairs vneezoo [внизу]

drain *(noun)* kanaleezatsee-ya [канализация]

drawing pin k-nopka [кнопка]

dress *(woman's)* platyeh [платье]

dressing *(for wound)* pyeryevyazka [перевязка]
 (for salad) preeprava [приправа]

dressing gown Halat [халат]

drink napeetak [напиток]
 (verb) peet [пить]
 would you like a drink? Hateetyeh shto-neebood viypeet? [хотите что-нибудь выпить?]
 I don't drink ya nyeh pyoo [я не пью]
 can you drink the water? vodoo moJna peet? [воду можно пить?]

drive: I've been driving all day ya vyes dyen za roolyom [я весь день за рулём]
 » *TRAVEL TIP: drive on the right and overtake on the left*

driver vadeetyel [водитель]

driving licence vadeetyelskee-yeh prava [водительские права]

drown: he's drowning on tonyet [он тонет]

drug *(medical)* lyekarstva [лекарство]
 (narcotic) narkoteek [наркотик]

drunk *(adj)* pyani [пьяный]

dry sooHoy [сухой]

dry-cleaner's Heemcheestka [химчистка]

due: when is the bus due? kagda preeHodeet aftoboos? [когда приходит автобус?]

during ftyechenee-yeh [в течение]

dust piyl [пыль]

duty-free *(adj)* dyootee-free [дьюти-фри]

  duty-free shop magazeen byesposhleenoy targovlee [магазин беспошлинной торговли]

dynamo deenama [динамо]

each: can we have one each? fsyeH pa adnamoo, paJalsta [всех по одному, пожалуйста]

  how much are they each? skolka sto-eet kaJdi? [сколько стоит каждый?]

ear ooHa [ухо]

  I have earache oo menya baleet ooHa [у меня болит ухо]

early rana [рано]

  we want to leave a day earlier miy Hateem oo-yeHat na dyen ransheh [мы хотим уехать на день раньше]

earring syerga [серьга]

east vastok [восток]

Easter PasHa [Пасха]

Eastern Europe Vastochna-ya Yevropa [Восточная Европа]

easy lyoHkee [лёгкий]

eat yest [есть]

  something to eat shto-neeboot pa-yest [что-нибудь поесть]

egg yItso [яйцо]

either: either ... or ... eelee ... eelee ... [или ... или ...]

  I don't like either mnyeh neekakoy nyeh nraveetsa [мне никакой не нравится]

elastic/elastic band rezeenka [резинка]

elbow lokat [локоть]

electric elyektreecheskee [электрический]

electric fire elyektrakameen [элекрокамин]

electrician elyektreek [электрик]

....

electricity elyektr*ee*chestva [электричество]

» *TRAVEL TIP: voltage is 220; you'll need a two-pin*
  continental adaptor

elegant elyeg*a*ntni [элегантный]

else: something else sht*o*-ta droog*o*-yeh [что-то
  другое]

   somewhere else gdy*e*h-neeboot vdroog*o*m
   my*e*styeh [где-нибудь в другом месте]

   who else? kto yesh*o*? [кто ещё?]

   or else *ee*lee [или]

embarassing nyeh-ood*o*bna [неудобно]

embassy pas*o*lstva [посольство]

emergency kreet*ee*cheska-ya seetoo-*a*tsee-ya
  [критическая ситуация]

empty poost*o*y [пустой]

enclose: I enclose ... ya preelag*a*-yoo ... [я
  прилагаю ...]

end kany*e*ts [конец]

   when does it end? kagd*a* kany*e*ts? [когда
   конец?]

engaged *(toilet/telephone)* zanyat*a* [занято]
   (man/woman) pamolvly*e*n/pamovly*e*na
   [помолвлен/помолвлена]

engagement ring obroch*a*lna-yeh kalts*o*
  [обручальное кольцо]

engine *(car)* dve*e*gatyel [двигатель]

   engine trouble prably*e*mi smat*o*ram
   [проблемы с мотором]

England *A*nglee-ya [Англия]

English *(adj)* angl*ee*skee [английский]
   (language) angl*ee*skee yaz*i*yk [английский
   язык]

   I'm English *(men/women)*
   ya angleech*a*neen/angleech*a*nka
   [я англичанин/англичанка]

enjoy: I enjoyed it very much mnyeh *o*chen
   panr*a*veelas [мне очень понравилось]

enlargement oovyelee*ee*chenee-yeh [увеличение]

enormous agr*o*mni [огромный]

enough: thank you, that's enough spas*ee*ba,
   eta dast*a*tachna [спасибо, это достаточно]

entertainment razvly*e*chenee-yeh

[развлечение]

entrance fHot [вход]
  (to house) padyezt [подъезд]
envelope kanvyert [конверт]
equipment abaroodavanee-yeh [оборудование]
  (for sport) snaryaJenee-yeh [снаряжение]
error asheepka [ошибка]
escalator eskalater [эскалатор]
especially asobyena [особенно]
essential asnavnoy [основной]
  it is essential that ... nyeh-abHadeema,
  shtobi ... [необходимо, чтобы ...]
ethnic natsee-onalni [национальный]
Europe Yevropa [Европа]
evacuate evakoo-eeravat [эвакуировать]
even: even here/even in Moscow daJeh
  zdyes/daJeh v Maskvyeh [даже здесь/даже в
  Москве]
evening vyecher [вечер]
  this evening svyevodnya vyecheram [сегодня
  вечером]
  good evening dobri vyecher [добрый вечер]
evening dress *(for man)* frak [фрак]
  (for woman) vyechernyeh-yeh platyeh [вечернее
  платье]
ever: have you ever been to ...? viy
  kagda-leeba bivalee v ...? [вы когда-либо
  бывали в ...?]
every kaJdi [каждый]
  every day kaJdi dyen [каждый день]
everyone fsyeh [все]
everything fsyo [всё]
everywhere fsyoodoo [всюду]
evidence sveedyetyelstva [свидетельство]
exact tochni [точный]
example preemyer [пример]
  for example napreemyer [например]
excellent atleechni [отличный]
except kromyeh [кроме]
  except me kromyeh menya [кроме меня]
excess baggage pyeryevyes bagaJa [перевес
  багажа]

....

exchange *(noun: money)* abmyen [обмен]
  (telephone) opyerater [оператор]
exciting oovlyekatyelni [увлекательный]
excursion ekskoorsee-ya [экскурсия]
excuse me! *(to get past/apologise)*
  eezveeneetyeh! [извините!]
  (to get attention) meenootachkoo! [минуточку!]
exhaust *(car)* viHlapna-ya trooba [выхлопная
  труба]
exhausted: I'm exhausted *(men/women)* ya
  ochen oostal/oostala [я очень устал/устала]
exit viyHot [выход]
expect: she's expecting ana v palaJenee [она в
  положении]
expensive: that's too expensive sleeshkam
  doraga [слишком дорого]
expert spetsee-aleest [специалист]
explain abyasneet [объяснить]
  would you explain that slowly?
  abyasneetyeh eta myedlyena, paJalsta
  [объясните это медленно, пожалуйста]
export *(noun)* ekspart [экспорт]
extra dapalneetyelni [дополнительный]
  an extra glass/day yesho adeen stakan/dyen
  [ещё один стакан/день]
  is that extra? eta za dapalneetyelnoo-yoo
  platoo? [это за дополнительную плату?]
extremely krInyeh [крайне]
eye glaz [глаз]
eyebrow brof [бровь]
eye shadow tyenee dlya vyek [тени для век]
face leetso [лицо]
fact fakt [факт]
factory zavod [завод]
Fahrenheit pa Faryengyaytoo [по Фаренгейту]
» *TRAVEL TIP: to convert F to C:* $F - 32 \times \dfrac{5}{9} = C$

Fahrenheit	5	23	32	50	70	86	98.4
centigrade	-15	-5	0	10	21	30	36.9

faint: she's fainted ana oopala vobmarak [она
  упала в обморок]
fair *(fun-)* yarmarka [ярмарка]

(commercial) viystafka [выставка]
   that's not fair eta nyespravyedleeva [это
   несправедливо]
fake *(noun)* falsheevka [фальшивка]
fall: he's fallen on oopal [он упал]
false loJni [ложный]
family syemya [семья]
fan *(mechanical)* vyenteelyater [вентилятор]
   (football, music etc) lyoobeetyel [любитель]
fan belt ryemyen vyenteelyatera [ремень
   вентилятора]
far dalyeko [далеко]
   is it far? eta dalyeko? [это далеко?]
fare *(travel)* sto-eemast pra-yezda [стоимость
   проезда]
farm fyerma [ферма]
   collective farm kalHoz [колхоз]
farther dalsheh [дальше]
fashion moda [мода]
fast biystri [быстрый]
   don't speak so fast gavareetyeh nyeh tak
   biystra [говорите не так быстро]
fat *(adj)* tolsti [толстый]
   (noun: on meat) Jeer [жир]
fatal fatalni [фатальный]
father atyets [отец]
fault nyedastatak [недостаток]
   it's not my fault *(men/women)* ya nyeh
   veenavat/veenavata [я не виноват/виновата]
faulty: this is faulty eta nyeh rabota-yet [это
не работает]
favourite *(adj)* lyoobeemi [любимый]
fax/fax machine faks [факс]
   fax *(verb)* atpraveet pa faksoo [отправить по
   факсу]
February fyevral [февраль]
fed up: I'm fed up mnyeh nada-yela [мне
надоело]
feel: I feel cold/hot/sad mnyeh Holadna/
   Jarka/groostna [мне холодно/жарко/грустно]
   I feel like ... mnyeh Hochetsa ... [мне хочется
   ...]

....

ferry parom [паром]

festival fyesteeval [фестиваль]

fetch: will you come and fetch me? viy zIdyotyeh za mnoy? [вы зайдёте за мной?]

few: only a few fsyevo nyeskolka [всего несколько]

   a few ... nyeskolka ... [несколько ...]

   a few days nyeskolka dnyay [несколько дней]

fiancé/fiancée JeneeH/nyevyesta [жених/невеста]

fiddle: it's a fiddle eta abman [это обман]

field polyeh [поле]

fifty-fifty poravnoo [поровну]

figs eenJeer [инжир]

figure *(number)* tseefra [цифра]

  (of person) figoora [фигура]

   I'm watching my figure ya slyeJoo za feegooroy [я слежу за фигурой]

fill: fill her up zaleevItyeh vyes bak [заливайте весь бак]

   to fill in a form zapolneet blank [заполнить бланк]

fillet feelyeh [филе]

film *(in cinema)* keenafeelm [кинофильм]

  (for camera) plyonka [плёнка]

   do you have this type of film? oo vas yest plyonka takoy markee? [у вас есть плёнка такой марки?]

filter: filter or non-filter? sfeeltram eelee byez? [с фильтром или без?]

find naHadeet [находить]

   if you find it yeslee viy nIdyotyeh [если вы найдёте]

   I've found a ... *(men/women)* ya nashol/nashla ... [я нашёл/нашла ...]

fine *(weather)* Haroshee [хороший]

   a 10-rouble fine shtraf dyesyat rooblyay [штраф десять рублей]

   OK, that's fine narmalna [нормально]

finger palyets [палец]

finish: I haven't finished *(men/women)* ya

yesho nyeh zakoncheel/zakoncheela [я ещё не закончил/закончила]

Finland Feenlyandee-ya [Финляндия]

fire: fire! paJar! [пожар!]

can we light a fire here? zdyes moJna razlaJeet kastyor? [здесь можно разложить костёр?]

fire brigade paJarna-ya kamanda [пожарная команда]

» *TRAVEL TIP: dial 01, say 'paJar'* [пожар] *and give your address and phone number*

fire extinguisher agnyetoosheetyel [огнетушитель]

first pyervi [первый]

I was first *(men)* ya biyl pyervim [я был первым]

(women) ya biyla pyervoy [я была первой]

first aid pyerva-ya pomosh [первая помощь]

first-aid kit aptyechka [аптечка]

first class *(excellent etc)* pyervi klas [первый класс]

» *TRAVEL TIP: first class on trains is 'es-veh'; there's no first class on domestic flights*

first name eemya [имя]

» *TRAVEL TIP: Russians address everyone, except friends and relatives, by their first name and patronymic (name of their father); foreigners usually get away with using the first name*

fish riyba [рыба]

fix: can you fix it? moJetyeh pacheeneet? [можете починить?]

fizzy gazeerovani [газированный]

flag flag [флаг]

flash *(photography)* fspiyshka [вспышка]

flat *(adj)* gladkee [гладкий]

(apartment) kvarteera [квартира]

this drink is flat etat napeetak viydaHsa [этот напиток выдохся]

I've got a flat tyre oo menya spoosteela sheena [у меня спустила шина]

flavour vkoos [вкус]

flea blaHa [блоха]

....

flies *(trousers)* sheereenka [ширинка]
flight palyot [полёт]
  flight number nomyer ryaysa [номер рейса]
float *(verb)* plavat [плавать]
floor pol [пол]
  (first, second etc) etaJ [этаж]
  on the second floor *(UK)* na tryetyem etaJeh
  [на третьем этаже]
  (Russia/US) na ftarom etaJeh [на втором этаже]
  which floor? na kakom etaJeh? [на каком
  этаже?]
  floor lady dyeJorna-ya [дежурная]
  » *TRAVEL TIP: acts as a receptionist for one or two*
  floors, hands out keys and provides tea
flower tsvyetok [цветок]
flu greep [грипп]
fly *(insect)* mooHa [муха]
foggy toomani [туманный]
folk dancing falklorni-yeh tantsi
  [фольклорные танцы]
folk music falklorna-ya moozika [фольклорная
  музыка]
follow slyedavat [следовать]
food yeda [еда]
food poisoning peeshevo-yeh atravlyenee-yeh
  [пищевое отравление]
fool doorak [дурак]
foot stoopnya [ступня]
  » *TRAVEL TIP: 1 foot = 30.1 cm = 0.3 metres*
football *(game)* footbol [футбол]
for dlya [для]
  this is for you eta dlya vas [это для вас]
  that's for me/her eta dlya menya/nyeh-yo
  [это для меня/неё]
forbidden zapryeshoni [запрещённый]
foreign eenastrani [иностранный]
foreigner *(man/woman)* eenastranyets/
  eenastranka [иностранец/иностранка]
foreign exchange abmyen valyooti [обмен
  валюты]
forget: I forget, I've forgotten *(men/women)*
  ya zabiyl/zabiyla [я забыл/забыла]

don't forget nyeh zab*oo*dtyeh [не забудьте]
fork v*ee*lka [вилка]
form *(document)* blank [бланк]
formal afeetsee-*a*lni [официальный]
fortnight dvyeh nyed*ye*lee [две недели]
forward: could you forward my mail?
paJ*a*lsta, pyeryeshl*ee*tyeh mnyeh ma-*yoo*
pochtoo [пожалуйста, перешлите мне мою
почту]
forwarding address *a*dryes dlya pyeryes*i*ylkee
[адрес для пересылки]
fracture pyeryel*o*m [перелом]
fragile Hr*oo*pkee [хрупкий]
fraud abm*a*n [обман]
free *(no charge)* byespl*a*tni [бесплатный]
(man/woman) svab*o*dyen/svab*o*dna
[свободен/свободна]
freight grooz [груз]
freshen up: I want to freshen up Hach*oo*
preevyest*ee* seb*ya* vpar*ya*dak [хочу привести
себя в порядок]
Friday py*a*tneetsa [пятница]
fridge Halad*ee*lneek [холодильник]
fried egg ya-*ee*chneetsa [яичница]
friend droog [друг]
friendly dr*oo*Jeskee [дружеский]
from: from London to Moscow at L*o*ndana da
Maskv*i*y [от Лондона до Москвы]
I'm from London/England ya eez Londana/
*A*nglee [я из Лондона/Англии]
where is it from? atk*oo*da eta? [откуда это?]
front *(noun)* pyeryedna-ya chast [передняя
часть]
in front of you py*e*ryed v*a*mee [перед вами]
in the front fpyery*e*d*ee* [впереди]
frost maroz [мороз]
frozen zam*yo*rshee [замёрзший]
the river is frozen over ryeka zam*yo*rzla
[река замёрзла]
I'm frozen *(men/women)* ya
pram*yo*rz/pram*yo*rzla naskvoz [я
промёрз/промёрзла насквозь]

••

fruit fr*oo*kti [фрукты]

fry Ja*ree*t [жарить]

　nothing fried neech*e*vo Jar*ye*nava [ничего жареного]

frying pan skavar*o*tka [сковородка]

fuel t*o*pleeva [топливо]

full p*o*lni [полный]

fun: it's fun *e*ta zab*a*vna [это забавно]

funny *(strange)* str*a*ni [странный]

　(comical) zab*a*vni [забавный]

fur myeH [мех]

　fur hat myeH*a*v*a*-ya sh*a*pka [меховая шапка]

furniture my*e*byel [мебель]

further d*a*lsheh [дальше]

fuse pryedaHran*ee*tyel [предохранитель]

fuss soo-y*e*ta [суета]

future boodoosheh-yeh [будущее]

　in the future vboodoosh*e*m [в будущем]

gale boor*ya* [буря]

gallon g*a*lon [галлон]

》》 *TRAVEL TIP: 1 gallon = 4.55 litres*

gallstones J*o*lchni-yeh k*a*mnee [жёлчные камни]

gamble eegr*a*t na dy*e*ngee [играть на деньги]

garage *(for repairs)* st*a*ntsee-ya tyeHabsl*oo*Jeevanee-ya [станция техобслуживания]

　(for petrol) byenzak*a*lonka [бензоколонка]

　(for parking) gar*a*J [гараж]

garden sad [сад]

garlic chesn*o*k [чеснок]

gas gas [газ]

　(petrol) benz*ee*n [бензин]

gas cylinder bal*o*n [баллон]

gay *(homosexual)* gamaseksoo-*a*lni [гомосексуальный]

gear *(car)* pyeryed*a*cha [передача]

　(equipment) vy*e*shee [вещи]

　I can't get it into gear nyeh mag*oo* pyeryeklyoo*ch*eet sk*o*rast [не могу переключить скорость]

gents mooJsk*o*y too-al*ye*t [мужской туалет]

get: will you get me a ...? preenyes*ee*tyeh, paJalsta ... [принесите, пожалуйста ...]

how do I get to the ferry? kak pap*a*st na parom? [как попасть на паром?]

when can I get it back? kagd*a* moJna zabr*a*t yev*o*? [когда можно забрать его?]

when do we get back? kagd*a* miy vyern*yo*msa? [когда мы вернёмся?]

where do I get off? gdyeh mnyeh viyHad*ee*t? [где мне выходить?]

where do I get a bus for ...? gdyeh astan*o*fka aft*o*boosa na ...? [где остановка автобуса на ...?]

have you got ...? oo vas yest ...? [у вас есть ...?]

ghetto blaster dvooHkas*ye*tneeH [двухкассетних]

gin jin [джин]

gin and tonic jin st*o*neekam [джин с тоником]

girl *(child)* dyev*a*chka [девочка]

(young woman) dyev*oo*shka [девушка]

girlfriend: my girlfriend ma-*ya* padr*oo*ga [моя подруга]

give dav*a*t [давать]

will you give me ...? d*I*tyeh, paJalsta ... [дайте, пожалуйста ...]

I gave it to him *(men/women)* ya dal/dala *e*ta yem*oo* [я дал/дала это ему]

glad rad [рад]

glandular fever vaspal*ye*nee-yeh Jel*yo*s [воспаление желёз]

glass styekl*o* [стекло]

(tumbler) stak*a*n [стакан]

(for wine) ry*oo*mka [рюмка]

a glass of water stak*a*n vad*iy* [стакан воды]

glasses achk*ee* [очки]

glue *(noun)* kl*ya*y [клей]

go *(on foot)* eedt*ee* [идти]

(by transport) ye*H*at [ехать]

I want to go to St Petersburg ya Hach*oo* pa-ye*H*at v Sankt Pyetyerboorg [я хочу

....

поехать в Санкт Петербург]

when does the bus go? kagda atHodeet
aftoboos? [когда отходит автобус?]

he's gone yevo zdyes nyet [его здесь нет]

I want to go *(leave: on foot)* ya Hachoo oo-eetee
[я хочу уйти]

can I have a go? moJna paprobavat? [можно
попробовать?]

goal *(sport)* gol [гол]

goat kaza [коза]

God bog [бог]

gold zolata [золото]

golf golf [гольф]

good Haroshee [хороший]

  good! Harasho! [хорошо!]

goodbye da sveedanee-ya [до свидания]
  (informal) paka [пока]

gooseberries kriJovneek [крыжовник]

gramme gram [грамм]

》 *TRAVEL TIP: 100 grammes = approx 3.5 oz*

grand *(building)* grandee-ozni [грандиозный]

granddaughter vnoochka [внучка]

grandfather dyedooshka [дедушка]

grandmother babooshka [бабушка]

grandson vnook [внук]

grapefruit graypfroot [грейпфрут]

grapefruit juice graypfrootavi sok
  [грейпфрутовый сок]

grapes veenagrad [виноград]

grass trava [трава]

grateful blagadarni [благодарный]

  I'm very grateful to you *(men/women)* ya vam
  ochen blagadaryen/blagadarna [я вам очень
  благодарен/благодарна]

gratitude blagadarnast [благодарность]

gravy so-oos [соус]

grease Jeer [жир]
  (for machinery) smaska [смазка]

greasy *(food)* Jeerni [жирный]

great *(large)* balshoy [большой]
  (major) vyeleekee [великий]

  great! prekrasna! [прекрасно!]

greedy Jadni [жадный]

green zyelyoni [зелёный]

greengrocer's avashnoy magazeen [овощной магазин]

grey syeri [серый]

grocer's pradavolstveni magazeen [продовольственный магазин]

ground *(area)* plashatka [площадка]
  on the ground na zemlyeh [на земле]

group groopa [группа]
  our group leader rookavadeetyel groopi [руководитель группы]
  I'm with the English group ya eez angleeskoy groopi [я из английской группы]

guarantee garantee-ya [гарантия]
  is there a guarantee? eta sgarantee-yay? [это с гарантией?]

guest *(man/woman)* gost/gostya [гость/гостья]

» *TRAVEL TIP: if you are invited to someone's home, you'll be treated to a lavish meal; it's customary to give useful and neatly-wrapped presents to your host or hostess*

guesthouse pansee-on [пансион]

» *TRAVEL TIP: until recently Russia only had hotels for foreign tourists but a few guesthouses are beginning to appear*

guide geed [гид]

guilty veenovni [виновный]

guitar geetara [гитара]

gum *(in mouth)* dyesna [десна]
  (for chewing) Jvachka [жвачка]

gun *(pistol)* peestolyet [пистолет]

gynaecologist geenyekolok [гинеколог]

hair volasi [волосы]

hairbrush shotka dlya valos [щётка для волос]

haircut streeJka [стрижка]

hairdresser's pareekmaHyerska-ya [парикмахерская]

hair grip shpeelka [шпилька]

hairspray lak dlya valos [лак для волос]

half palaveena [половина]
  a half portion palportsee [полпорции]

half an hour polchasa [полчаса]
ham vyetcheena [ветчина]
hamburger gamboorger [гамбургер]
hammer malatok [молоток]
hand rooka [рука]
handbag soomachka [сумочка]
handbrake roochnoy tormaz [ручной тормоз]
handkerchief nasavoy platok [носовой
платок]
handle (*noun*) roochka [ручка]
hand luggage roochna-ya klat [ручная кладь]
handmade: this is handmade eta roochna-ya
rabota [это ручная работа]
handsome kraseevi [красивый]
hanger vyeshalka [вешалка]
hangover paHmyelyeh [похмелье]
YOU MAY WANT TO SAY ...
my head is killing me ochen baleet galava
[очень болит голова]
happen: I don't know how it happened ya
nyeh zna-yoo, kak eta paloocheelas [я не знаю,
как это получилось]
what's happening/happened? shto
sloocheelas? [что случилось?]
happy shastleevi [счастливый]
harbour port [порт]
hard tvyordi [твёрдый]
(*difficult*) troodni [трудный]
push hard talkI seelnyeh-yeh [толкай
сильнее]
hard-boiled egg yItso fkrootoo-yoo [яйцо
вкрутую]
hard currency valyoota [валюта]
hard-currency shop valyootni magazeen
[валютный магазин]
» *TRAVEL TIP: the choice of goods in a Beriozka or
other hard-currency shop is much better than in
a rouble shop but the prices are higher*
hardware shop HazyIstvyeni magazeen
[хозяйственный магазин]
harm (*noun*) vryed [вред]
hat (*with/without flaps*) shapka/shlyapa

[шапка/шляпа]

hate: I hate ... ya nyenave*e*Joo ...
[я ненавижу ...]

have: can I have ...? d*I*tyeh, paJ*a*lsta ... [дайте,
пожалуйста ...]

  can I have some more? m*o*Jna yesh*o*? [можно
  ещё?]

  I have no ... oo men*ya* nyet ... [у меня нет ...]

  do you have any cigars/a map? oo vas yest
  seeg*a*ri/k*a*rta? [у вас есть сигары/карта?]

  I have to leave tomorrow mnyeh n*a*da
  oo-*ye*Hat z*a*ftra [мне надо уехать завтра]

hayfever s*y*ena-ya leeH*a*ratka [сенная
лихорадка]

he on [он]

head gal*a*va [голова]

headache galavn*a*-ya bol [головная боль]

headlights pyer*ye*dnee-yeh f*a*ri [передние
фары]

head waiter myetrd*a*t*y*el [метрдотель]

health zd*a*rov*y*eh [здоровье]

  your health! v*a*sheh zd*a*rov*y*eh! [ваше
  здоровье!]

healthy zdar*o*vi [здоровый]

hear: I can't hear ya nyeh sl*i*yshoo [я не
слышу]

hearing aid slooH*a*v*o*y apar*a*t [слуховой
аппарат]

heart s*y*erdtseh [сердце]

heart attack eenf*a*rkt [инфаркт]

heat J*a*ra [жара]

heating atapl*y*enee-yeh [отопление]

heavy tyaJ*o*li [тяжёлый]

heel *(of foot)* p*ya*tka [пятка]

  (of shoe) kabl*oo*k [каблук]

  could you put new heels on these? paJ*a*lsta,
  past*a*vtyeh sy*oo*d*a* nab*o*ykee [пожалуйста,
  поставьте сюда набойки]

height *(of person)* rost [рост]

  (of building etc) visat*a* [высота]

hello zdr*a*svoot*ye*h [здравствуйте]

  (informal) preev*ye*t [привет]

....

(on telephone) allo [алло]

help *(noun)* pomosh [помощь]

    can you help me? pama*gee*tyeh mnyeh,
paJalsta [помогите мне, пожалуйста]

    help! na pomosh! [на помощь!]

her: I like her mnyeh ana nraveetsa [мне она
нравится]

    with her snyay [с ней]

    to her yay [ей]

    her ... yeh-*yo* ... [её ...]

    it's her bag *e*ta yeh-*yo* soomachka [это её
сумочка]

    that's/it's hers *e*ta yeh-*yo* [это её]

here zdyes [здесь]

    come here eed*ee*tyeh syood*a* [идите сюда]

high visokee [высокий]

hill gar*a* [гора]

him: I don't know him ya yev*o* nyeh zn*a*-yoo [я
его не знаю]

    with him sneem [с ним]

    to him yem*oo* [ему]

hire vzyat napra*ka*t [взять напрокат]

his yevo [его]

    it's his drink/it's his *e*ta yevo stakan/*e*ta yevo
[это его стакан/это его]

hit: he hit me on ood*a*reel menya [он ударил
меня]

hitch-hike pootyeshestvavat aftast*o*pam
[путешествовать автостопом]

» *TRAVEL TIP: not recommended for safety reasons*

hold *(verb)* dyerJat [держать]

hole dira [дыра]

holiday prazdneek [праздник]

    I'm on holiday ya votpooskyeh [я в отпуске]

    holiday cottage lyetnee domeek [летний
домик]

home dom [дом]

    I want to go home ya Hachoo damoy [я хочу
домой]

    at home *(in the house)* doma [дома]

    (in one's own country) na rodeenyeh [на родине]

homesick: I'm homesick ya taskoo-yoo pa

rodeenyeh [я тоскую по родине]

honest chestni [честный]

honestly? syeryozna? [серьёзно?]

honey myod [мёд]

honeymoon myedovi myesyats [медовый месяц]

hope *(noun)* nadyeJda [надежда]

  I hope that ... ya nadyeh-yoos, shto ... [я надеюсь, что ...]

  I hope so/I hope not navyerna-yeh da/navyerna-yeh nyet [наверное да/наверное нет]

horn *(car)* seegnal [сигнал]

horrible ooJasni [ужасный]

hors d'œuvre zakooska [закуска]

horse loshat [лошадь]

hospital balneetsa [больница]

» *TRAVEL TIP: state hospitals are for Russians only, although in remote areas foreigners may be admitted; in main cities you'll be charged in a hospital for foreigners; insurance is essential; medical evacuation insurance is recommended*

host Hazya-een [хозяин]

hostess Hazylka [хозяйка]

hot *(to touch)* garyachee [горячий]
  (weather) Jarkee [жаркий]

hotel gasteeneetsa [гостиница]

  hotel card kartachka gostya [карточка гостья]

hour chas [час]

house dom [дом]

housewife damaHazylka [домохозяйка]

how kak [как]

  how many? skolka? [сколько?]

  how much? *(price)* skolka sto-eet? [сколько стоит?]

  how often? kak chasta? [как часто?]

  how often do the trains go? *(per day/per hour)* skolka pa-yezdof vdyen/vchas? [сколько поездов в день/в час?]

  how long does it take? *(flight/other transport)* skolka lyetyet/yeHat? [сколько лететь/ехать?]

how long have you been here? viy zdyes davn*o*? [вы здесь давно?]

how are you? kak dyel*a*? [как дела?]

YOU MAY THEN HEAR ...

narm*a*lna *OK*

vpary*a*dkyeh *I'm fine*

Harasho *fine*

humid vl*a*Jni [влажный]

humour *yoo*mer [юмор]

haven't you got a sense of humour? oo vas yest choostva *yoo*mara? [у вас есть чувство юмора?]

hundredweight

» *TRAVEL TIP: 1 cwt = 50.8 kilos*

Hungary V*y*engree-ya [Венгрия]

hungry: I'm (not) hungry ya (nyeh) Hach*oo* yest [я (не) хочу есть]

hurry: I'm in a hurry ya tarapl*yoo*s [я тороплюсь]

please hurry! paskar*yeh*-yeh, paJ*a*lsta! [поскорее, пожалуйста!]

hurt: it hurts b*o*lna [больно]

my leg hurts oo men*ya* bal*ee*t nag*a* [у меня болит нога]

husband moosh [муж]

hydrofoil geedraf*oy*l [гидрофойл]

I ya [я]

I am English *(men/women)* ya angleech*a*neen/angleech*a*nka [я англичанин/англичанка]

I am a teacher *(men/women)* ya ooch*ee*tyel/ooch*ee*tyelneetsa [я учитель/учительница]

ice lyot [лёд]

with lots of ice pab*o*lsheh lda [побольше льда]

ice cream maroJena-yeh [мороженое]

ice hockey Hak*ya*y s-sh*l*boy [хоккей с шайбой]

ice rink kat*o*k [каток]

ice skates kank*ee* [коньки]

ice skating kat*a*nee-yeh na kank*a*H [катание на коньках]

icon eekona [икона]
icy lyedyan*oy* [ледяной]
idiot eedee-ot [идиот]
» *TRAVEL TIP: one of the strongest swearwords used in public: be careful when you feel like using it; if in doubt say the more neutral 'eedee-ateezm'* [идиотизм] *which means 'idiocy'*
if *y*eslee [если]
ignition (*car*) zaJeeganee-yeh [зажигание]
ill baln*oy* [больной]
  I feel ill mnyeh ploHa [мне плохо]
illegal nyezakoni [незаконный]
illegible nyerazborcheevi [неразборчивый]
illness bal*y*ezn [болезнь]
immediately nyem*y*edlyena [немедленно]
import (*noun*) *ee*mport [импорт]
important va*J*ni [важный]
  it's very important *e*ta *o*chen va*J*na [это очень важно]
import duty tamoJena-ya p*o*shleena (na v-voz) [таможенная пошлина (на ввоз)]
impossible nyevazm*o*Jni [невозможный]
impressive fpyechatl*ya*-yooshee [впечатляющий]
improve oolo*o*chshat [улучшать]
  I want to improve my Russian ya Hach*oo* loochsheh gavar*ee*t pa-r*oo*skee [я хочу лучше говорить по-русски]
in: in England v*A*nglee [в Англии]
  in English pa-angl*ee*skee [по-английски]
inch dyoom [дюйм]
» *TRAVEL TIP: 1 inch = 2.54 cm*
include fklyooch*a*t [включать]
  does that include breakfast? z*a*ftrak fklyoochon vsto-eemast? [завтрак включён в стоимость?]
inclusive fklyooch*ee*tyelna [включительно]
incompetent nyekampyet*y*entni [некомпетентный]
inconsiderate nyeh-abd*oo*mani [необдуманный]
incredible nyevyera-*ya*tni [невероятный]

indecent nyepreeleechni [неприличный]
independent nyezaveeseemi [независимый]
India Eendee-ya [Индия]
Indian (adj) eendeeskee [индийский]
indicator ookazatyel [указатель]
indigestion eezJoga [изжога]
indoors fpamyeshenee [в помещении]
industry pramiyshlyenast [промышленность]
infection zaraJenee-yeh [заражение]
infectious eenfyektsee-oni [инфекционный]
inflation eenflyatsee-ya [инфляция]
informal nyeh-afeetsee-alni [неофициальный]
information eenfarmatsee-ya [информация]
  do you have any information in English about …? oo vas yest shto-neebood pa-angleeskee o …? [у вас есть что-нибудь по-английски о …?]
  where is there an information office? gdyeh spravachna-yeh byooro? [где справочное бюро?]
inhabitant Jeetyel [житель]
injection eenyektsee-ya [инъекция]
injured ranyeni [раненый]
  he's been injured on ranyen [он ранен]
injury rana [рана]
innocent nyeveeni [невинный]
insect nasyekoma-yeh [насекомое]
insect repellent sryedstva ot nasyekomiн [средство от насекомых]
inside vnootree [внутри]
insist: I insist ya nasta-eeva-yoo [я настаиваю]
insomnia byesoneetsa [бессонница]
instant coffee rastvareemi kofeh [растворимый кофе]
instead: instead of … vmyesta … [вместо …]
  can I have that one instead? moJna zamyeneet na eta? [можно заменить на это?]
insulating tape eezalyenta [изолента]
insult askarblyenee-yeh [оскорбление]
insurance straHofka [страховка]
intelligent oomni [умный]
interesting eentyeryesni [интересный]

international myeJdoonarodni
[международный]

interpret: would you interpret for us? viy
moJetyeh biyt nasheem pyeryevodcheekam?
[вы можете быть нашим переводчиком?]

interpreter (*man/woman*) pyeryevodcheek/
pyeryevodcheetsa [переводчик/ переводчица]

into v [в]

introduce: can I introduce ...? razryesheetyeh
paznakomeet ... [разрешите познакомить ...]

invalid (*noun*) eenvaleed [инвалид]

invitation preeglashenee-yeh [приглашение]
thank you for the invitation spaseeba za
preeglashenee-yeh [спасибо за приглашение]

invite: can I invite you to dinner? moJna
preeglaseet vas na ooJeen? [можно
пригласить вас на ужин?]

Iran Eeran [Иран]

Ireland Eerlandee-ya [Ирландия]

Irish eerlandskee [ирландский]

iron (*noun: for clothes*) ootyoog [утюг]
will you iron this for me? pagladtyeh eta,
paJalsta [погладьте это, пожалуйста]

island ostraf [остров]

it: it is ... eta ... [это ...]

itch (*noun*) zood [зуд]
it itches cheshetsa [чешется]

itemize: would you itemize it for me? moJna
padrobni shot? [можно подробный счёт?]

jack (*car repair*) damkrat [домкрат]

jacket (*suit*) peedJak [пиджак]
(*blouson*) Jakyet [жакет]

jam varyenyeh [варенье]
traffic jam propka [пропка]

January yanvar [январь]

jaw chelyoost [челюсть]

jealous ryevneevi [ревнивый]

jeans jeensi [джинсы]

jellyfish myedooza [медуза]

jetty preestan [пристань]

jewellery yoovyeleerni-yeh eezdyeli-ya
[ювелирные изделия]

....

job rabota [работа]
    just the job to, shto nooJna [то, что нужно]
joke *(noun)* shootka [шутка]
    you must be joking! nyeh moJet biyt! [не может быть!]
journey pootyeshestvee-yeh [путешествие]
    have a good journey! schastleevava pootee! [счастливого пути!]
July ee-yool [июль]
jumper sveetyer [свитер]
junction *(of roads)* pyeryekryostak [перекрёсток]
June ee-yoon [июнь]
junk *(rubbish)* staryo [старьё]
just: just two *(only)* tolka dva [только два]
    put it just there palaJee vot tooda [положи вот туда]
    it's just there vot tam [вот там]
    not just now nyeh syaychas [не сейчас]
    just now *(a little while ago)* savsyem nyedavna [совсем недавно]
    that's just right eta fsami raz [это в самый раз]
keen: I'm very keen to ... mnyeh ochen Hochetsa ... [мне очень хочется ...]
    I'm not keen mnyeh nyeh Hochetsa [мне не хочется]
keep: can I keep it? eta mnyeh nasavsyem? [это мне насовсем?]
    you keep it astav syebyeh [оставь себе]
    keep the change zdachee nyeh nada [сдачи не надо]
kettle chJneek [чайник]
key klyooch [ключ]
KGB 'ka-ge-be' [КГБ]
kidneys pochkee [почки]
kill *(verb)* oobeet [убить]
kilo keelagram [килограмм]
» *TRAVEL TIP: conversion:* $\frac{kilos}{5} \times 11 = pounds$

kilos	1	1.5	5	6	7	8	9
pounds	2.2	3.3	11	13.2	15.4	17.6	19.8

....

kilometre keelamyetr [километр]

» *TRAVEL TIP: conversion:* $\frac{kilometres}{5} \times 11 = miles$

kilometres	1	5	10	20	50	100
miles		0.62	3.11	6.2	12.4	31	62

kind: that's very kind of you balsho-yeh vam spaseeba [большое вам спасибо]

kiosk kee-osk [киоск]

kiss (noun) patseloo-ee [поцелуй]

kitchen kooHnya [кухня]

knee kalyena [колено]

knickers trooseekee [трусики]

knife nosh [нож]

knock (verb) stoochat [стучать]

there's a knocking noise from the engine mator stoocheet [мотор стучит]

know znat [знать]

I don't know ya nyeh zna-yoo [я не знаю]

Kremlin Kryeml [Кремль]

kvas kvas [квас]

» *TRAVEL TIP: drinking out of vending machines is not recommended unless using your own cup*

label (noun) yarliyk [ярлык]

laces (shoe) shnoorkee [шнурки]

ladies (toilet) Jenskee too-alyet [женский туалет]

lady dama [дама]

lager svyetla-yeh peeva [светлое пиво]

lamb (meat) baraneena [баранина]

lamp lampa [лампа]

lamppost fanarni stolp [фонарный столб]

lampshade abaJoor [абажур]

land (noun: not sea) soosha [суша]

lane (country road) daroga [дорога]

(on motorway) ryad [ряд]

language yaziyk [язык]

large balshoy [большой]

laryngitis lareengeet [ларингит]

last paslyednee [последний]

last year/last week vproshlam gadoo/na proshlay nyedyelyeh [в прошлом году/на прошлой неделе]

....

last night fchera nochoo [вчера ночью]

at last! nakanyets! [наконец!]

late: sorry I'm late eezveeneetyeh za apazdanee-yeh [извините за опоздание]

it's a bit late nyemnoga pozdna [немного поздно]

please hurry, I'm late patarapeetyes, ya apazdiva-yoo [поторопитесь, я опаздываю]

at the latest sama-yeh pozdnyeh-yeh [самое позднее]

later poJeh [позже]

see you later da skorava [до скорого]

laugh (verb) smyeh-yatsa [смеяться]

lavatory too-alyet [туалет]

law zakon [закон]

lawyer yooreest [юрист]

laxative slabeetyelna-yeh [слабительное]

lazy lyeneevi [ленивый]

lead-free petrol byenzeen byez dabavlyenee-ya sveentsa [бензин без добавления свинца]; see **petrol**

leaf leest [лист]

leak: there's a leak zdyes tyechot [здесь течёт]

learn: I want to learn ... ya Hachoo oocheetsa ... [я хочу учиться ...]

least: not in the least nee vko-yem sloochay [ни в коем случае]

at least pa krinyeh myeryeh [по крайней мере]

leather koJa [кожа]

leave: we're leaving tomorrow miy oo-yeJa-yem zaftra [мы уезжаем завтра]

when does the bus leave? kagda atHodeet aftoboos? [когда отходит автобус?]

I left two shirts in my room ya zabiyl dvyeh roobashkee vnomyeryeh [я забыл две рубашки в номере]

can I leave this here? moJna eta zdyes astaveet? [можно это здесь оставить?]

left lyevi [левый]

on the left slyeva [слева]

left-handed lyevsha [левша]

left luggage office kamyera Hranyenee-ya
[камера хранения]

leg naga [нога]

legal: is it legal? eta zakona? [это законно?]

lemon leemon [лимон]

lemonade leemanad [лимонад]

lend: will you lend me your …? adalJeetyeh,
paJalsta, vash … [одолжите, пожалуйста,
ваш …]

Leningrad Lyeneengrad [Ленинград]

» *TRAVEL TIP: the city's original name, St
Petersburg, has been restored*

lens *(camera)* abyekteef [объектив]

less myensheh [меньше]

    less than that myensheh, chem zdyes
[меньше, чем здесь]

let: let me help razryesheetyeh vam pamoch
[разрешите вам помочь]

    let me go! poosteetyeh menya! [пустите
меня!]

    will you let me off here? moJna mnyeh zdyes
viytee? [можно здесь выйти?]

    let's go pashlee [пошли]

letter peesmo [письмо]

    are there any letters for me? yest peesma
dlya menya? [есть письма для меня?]

letterbox pachtovi yasheek [почтовый ящик]

lettuce salat [салат]

level-crossing pyeryeh-yezd [переезд]

library beeblee-atyeka [библиотека]

licence *(for fishing, gun etc)* leetsensee-ya
[лицензия]

lid kriyshka [крышка]

lie *(untruth)* loJ [ложь]

    can I/he/she lie down for a bit? moJna
palyeJat atdaHnoot? [можно полежать
отдохнуть?]

life Jeezn [жизнь]

lifebelt spasatyelni po-yas [спасательный пояс]

lifeboat spasatyelna-ya shlyoopka
[спасательная шлюпка]

lifeguard tyelaHraneetyel [телохранитель]

....

life jacket spas*a*tyelni Jeel*y*et [спасательный жилет]

lift: do you want a lift? vas padvyes*tee*? [вас подвезти?]

   could you give me a lift? mo*Jetyeh men*ya padvyes*tee*? [можете меня подвезти?]

   the lift isn't working leeft nyeh rabota-yet [лифт не работает]

light[1] svyet [свет]

   the lights aren't working (car) f*a*ri nyeh rabota-yoot [фары не работают]

   have you got a light? oo vas nyet sp*ee*chek? [у вас нет спичек?]

   when it gets light kagda nastoopeet ootra [когда наступит утро]

light[2] *(not heavy)* lyoHkee [лёгкий]

light bulb l*a*mpachka [лампочка]

light meter ekspanomyetr [экспонометр]

like: would you like ...? Hat*ee*tyeh ...? [хотите ...?]

   I'd like a/to ... mnyeh H*o*chetsa ... [мне хочется ...]

   I like it mnyeh nr*a*veetsa [мне нравится]

   I like you viy mnyeh nr*a*veetyes [вы мне нравитесь]

   I don't like it mnyeh nyeh nr*a*veetsa [мне не нравится]

   what's it like? *e*ta kak? [это как?]

   do it like this *e*ta nada zdyelat tak [это надо сделать так]

lime *(cordial)* leemoni seer*o*p [лимонный сироп]

line *(telephone etc)* leenee-ya [линия]

lip gooba [губа]

lip salve geegee-yen*ee*cheska-ya pam*a*da [гигиеническая помада]

lipstick goobn*a*-ya pam*a*da [губная помада]

liqueur leek*y*or [ликёр]

list *(noun)* sp*ee*sak [список]

listen! paslooshIt*y*eh! [послушайте!]

litre leetr [литр]

  » *TRAVEL TIP: 1 litre = 1.75 pints = 0.22 gals*

little m*a*lyenkee [маленький]
  a little ice/a little more nyemn*o*ga
  l*d*a/pab*o*lsheh [немного льда/побольше]
  just a little choot-choot [чуть-чуть]
live Jeet [жить]
  I live in Glasgow ya Jeev*oo* v 'Glasgow' [я
  живу в Глазго]
  where do you live? gdyeh viy Jeev*y*otyeh?
  [где вы живёте?]
liver *(in body)* pyechen [печень]
  (food) pech*o*nka [печёнка]
loaf booH*a*nka [буханка]
lobster am*a*r [омар]
local: could we try a local wine? m*o*Jna
  paprob*a*vat my*e*stnava v*ee*na? [можно
  попробовать местного вина?]
  a local restaurant my*e*stni ryestar*a*n
  [местный ресторан]
lock: the lock's broken zam*o*k slam*a*lsa [замок
  сломался]
  I've locked myself out *(men/women)* ya
  slooch*i*na zaHlopn*oo*l/zaHlopn*oo*la dvyer [я
  случайно захлопнул/захлопнула дверь]
lonely ad*ee*n*o*kee [одинокий]
long dl*ee*ni [длинный]
  we'd like to stay longer miy biy Hat*y*el*ee*
  zadyerJ*a*tsa zdyes [мы бы хотели
  задержаться здесь]
  that was long ago *e*ta b*i*yla davn*o* [это было
  давно]
loo: where's the loo? gdyeh too-al*y*et? [где
  туалет?]
look: you look tired oo vas oost*a*li veed [у вас
  усталый вид]
  I'm looking forward to ... ya ochen Jd*oo* ... [я
  очень жду ...]
  I'm looking for ... ya ees*h*oo ... [я ищу ...]
  look out! astar*o*Jna! [осторожно!]
loose: this button/handle is loose *e*ta
  p*oo*gav*ee*tsa/r*oo*chka balt*a*-yetsa [это
  пуговица/ручка болтается]
lorry grooz*a*veek [грузовик]

....

lorry driver vad*ee*tyel groozaveek*a* [водитель грузовика]

lose tyer*y*at [терять]

I've lost my bag *(men/women)* ya patyer*y*al/patyer*y*ala s*oo*mkoo [я потерял/потеряла сумку]

excuse me, I'm lost *(men/women)* kaJetsa, ya zablood*ee*elas/zablood*ee*elas [кажется, я заблудился/заблудилась]

lost property office by*oo*ro naHodak [бюро находок]

lot: a lot, lots mn*o*ga [много]

a lot of bread/wine mn*o*ga Hl*y*eba/veen*a* [много хлеба/вина]

a lot more expensive gar*a*zda daroJeh [гораздо дороже]

lotion las*y*on [лосьон]

loud gr*o*mkee [громкий]

louder gr*o*mcheh [громче]

love: I love you ya vas ly*oo*obly*oo* [я вас люблю]

do you love me? tiy men*y*a ly*oo*obeesh? [ты меня любишь?]

he's in love on vly*oo*obly*o*n [он влюблён]

I love this vodka mn*y*eh nr*a*veetsa *e*ta v*o*dka [мне нравится эта водка]

lovely zamyech*a*tyelni [замечательный]

low n*ee*zkee [низкий]

luck s*oo*db*a* [судьба]

good luck! Jel*a*-yoo oospy*e*Ha! [желаю успеха!]

lucky: you're lucky vam vy*e*zyot [вам везёт]

that's lucky! vot Harasho! [вот хорошо!]

luggage bag*a*sh [багаж]

luggage locker aftamat*ee*cheska-ya k*a*myera Hran*y*enee-ya [автоматическая камера хранения]

lumbago ly*oo*mb*a*ga [люмбаго]

lump *(in body)* op*oo*kHal [опухоль]

lunch ab*y*ed [обед]

lungs ly*o*Hkee-yeh [лёгкие]

luxurious rask*o*shni [роскошный]

luxury r*o*skash [роскошь]

mad soomashedshee [сумасшедший]

made-to-measure sdyelan pa zakazoo [сделан по заказу]

magazine Joornal [журнал]

magnificent vyeleekalyepni [великолепный]

maiden name dyeveecha fameelee-ya [девичья фамилия]

mail *(noun)* pochta [почта]

main road asnavnaya daroga [основная дорога]

make dyelat [делать]

will we make it in time? miy oospyeh-yem? [мы успеем?]

made in Russia sdyelana v Rasee [сделано в России]

make-up kazmyeteeka [косметика]

man mooJcheena [мужчина]

manager admeeneestrater [администратор]

can I see the manager? pazaveetyeh admeeneestratera, paJalsta [позовите администратора, пожалуйста]

manners pavyedyenee-yeh [поведение]

many mnogee-yeh [многие]

map karta [карта]

a map of Russia/Moscow karta Rasee/Maskviy [карта России/Москвы]

March mart [март]

margarine margareen [маргарин]

mark: there's a mark on it zdyes pyatno [здесь пятно]

market/market place riynak [рынок]

marmalade marmyelad [мармелад]

married *(man/woman)* Jenat/zamooJem [женат/замужем]

marvellous zamyechatyelni [замечательный]

mascara toosh dlya ryesneets [тушь для ресниц]

massage massaJ [массаж]

mat kovreek [коврик]

match speechka [спичка]

a box of matches karopka speechek [коробка

спичек]

football match footbolni match [футбольный матч]

material tkan [ткань]

matter: it doesn't matter nyeva*J*na [неважно]

  what's the matter? fchom d*y*ela? [в чём дело?]

mattress matr*a*s [матрас]

maximum m*a*kseemoom [максимум]

May mI [май]

may: may I have …? d*I*tyeh mnyeh, pa*J*alsta … [дайте мне, пожалуйста …]

maybe mo*J*et biyt [может быть]

mayonnaise mI-an*y*ez [майонез]

me: for me dlya men*y*a [для меня]

  can you hear me? viy men*y*a sl*i*ysheetyeh? [вы меня слышите?]

  please give it to me d*I*tyeh eta mnyeh, pa*J*alsta [дайте это мне, пожалуйста]

meal yed*a* [еда]

mean: what does this mean? shto *e*ta zn*a*cheet? [что это значит?]

measles kor [корь]

  German measles krasnoo*H*a [краснуха]

measurements razm*y*eri [размеры]

meat m*y*asa [мясо]

mechanic: is there a mechanic here? zdyes yest myeH*a*neek? [здесь есть механик?]

medicine myedeetse*e*na [медицина]

meet fstry*e*teetsa [встретиться]

  when can we meet again? kagd*a* miy snova fstry*e*teemsa? [когда мы снова встретимся?]

  pleased to meet you *(men/women)* rad/r*a*da paznak*o*meetsa [рад/рада познакомиться]

  YOU MAY HEAR:

  paznak*o*mtyes … *please meet …*

  *o*chen pree-*y*atna *nice to meet you*

meeting *(with several people)* savy*e*shanee-yeh [совещание]

  (with one person) fstry*e*cha [встреча]

melon d*i*ynya [дыня]

melt ta-yat [таять]

member chlen [член]
  how do I become a member? kak fstoopeet vetoo arganeezatsee-yoo? [как вступить в эту организацию?]
men mooJcheeni [мужчины]
mend: can you mend this? eta moJna pacheeneet? [это можно починить?]
mention: don't mention it nyeh-za-shto [не за что]
menu myenyoo [меню]
  can I have the menu, please? dItyeh mnyeh myenyoo, paJalsta [дайте мне меню, пожалуйста]
mess byesparyadak [беспорядок]
message: are there any messages for me? mnyeh shto-neebood pyeryedavalee? [мне что-нибудь передавали?]
  can I leave a message for ...? moJetyeh pyeryedat ...? [можете передать ...?]
metre myetr [метр]
» *TRAVEL TIP: 1 metre = 39.37 inches = 1.09 yds*
midday poldyen [полдень]
middle syeryedeena [середина]
  in the middle pasyeryedeenyeh [посередине]
midnight polnach [полночь]
might: I might be late ya, vyera-yatna, zadyerJoos [я, вероятно, задержусь]
  he might have gone on, vyera-yatna, ooshol [он, вероятно, ушёл]
migraine meegryen [мигрень]
mild myagkee [мягкий]
mile meelya [миля]
» *TRAVEL TIP: conversion:* $\frac{miles}{5} \times 8 = kilometres$

miles	0.5	1	3	5	10	50	100
kilometres	0.8	1.6	4.8	8	16	80	160

military va-yeni [военный]
milk malako [молоко]
milkshake malochni kaktyayl [молочный коктейль]
millimetre meeleemyetr [миллиметр]
minced meat farsh [фарш]

....

ЗАКУСКИ   ZAKOOSKEE   STARTERS

белуга   byelooga
  white sturgeon
блиной с икрой   bleeniy seekroy
  pancakes with caviar
блиной со сметаной   bleeniy sa-smetanoy
  pancakes with soured cream
буженина   booJeneena
  pork baked with garlic and pepper
винегрет   veenyegryet
  *potatoes, beetroot, peas, pickles and other
  vegetables in vinegar and oil dressing*
жюльен из шампиньонов   Joolyen eez
  shampeenyonav
  mushrooms in sour cream
заливная рыба   zaleevna-ya riyba
  *fish in aspic with hard-boiled eggs and
  vegetables*
икра красная   eekra krasna-ya
  red caviar
икра чёрная   eekra chorna-ya
  black caviar
салат   salat
  salad
салат из огурцов   salat eez agoortsof
  cucumber salad with soured cream
салат из помидоров   salat eez pameedorav
  tomato salad with soured cream
севрюга   syevryooga
  *delicious kind of smoked sturgeon served hot or
  cold*
селёдка малосольная   syelyodka malasolna-ya
  pickled herring
сёмга   syomga
  smoked salmon
шпроты   shproti
  sprats
язык   yaziyk
  boiled calf's tongue served with crisp vegetables

СУПЫ	SOOPI	SOUPS

борщ   borsh
thick beetroot and cabbage soup

бульон   boolyon
broth

бульон с фрикадельками   boolyon
sfreekadyelkamee
broth with meat and rice balls

грибной суп   greebnoy soop
mushroom soup with onions, served with soured cream

овощной суп   avashnoy soop
vegetable soup

уха   ooHa
thick fish soup

щи   shee
sauerkraut-based soup

MAIN DISHES

бифштекс   beefshtyeks
steak

вареники   varyeneekee
Russian ravioli filled with whole cherries or tvorog (Russian cottage cheese)

грибное рагу   greebno-yeh ragoo
mushroom and potato stew

гуляш   goolyash
goulash – beef or veal stewed in soured cream sauce

карп печёный   karp pyechoni
carp baked in cream sauce

котлеты   katlyeti
chops

котлеты по-киевски   katlyeti pa-kee-yevskee
chicken Kiev – stuffed chicken leg fried in breadcrumbs

овощное рагу   avashno-yeh ragoo
vegetable stew

пельмени   pelmyenee
Russian ravioli usually served with melted butter or soured cream

телятина   tyelyateena
  veal
телячьи отбивные   telyachee atbeevniy-yeh
  veal chops
шашлык   shashliyk
  pieces of marinated meat barbecued on skewers,
  served with onions and tomatoes

RUSSIAN SPECIALITIES

блинчики   bleencheekee
  small pancakes served with either soured cream
  or jam
каша   kasha
  porridge, made from either buckwheat, semolina
  or oatmeal and eaten at breakfast
компот   kampot
  stewed fruit in fruit juice
солёные огурцы   salyoni-yeh agoortsiy
  salted cucumbers
пирожки с капустой   peeraJkee skapoostoy
  small cabbage pies, eaten as a snack or for lunch
пирожки с мясом   peeraJkee smyasam
  small meat pies, eaten as a snack or for lunch

СЛАДКИЕ БЛЮДА
SLADKEE-YEH BLYOODA   SWEETS

варенье   varyenyeh
  preserves containing whole berries or large
  pieces of fruit
ватрушка   vatrooshka
  cheesecake
мороженое   maroJena-yeh
  ice cream
пирожное   peeroJna-yeh
  any kind of small pie or pastry
торт   tort
  cake

mind: I've changed my mind (men/women)
ya pyeryedoomal/pyeryedoomala
[я передумал/передумала]
I don't mind Harasho [хорошо]
do you mind if I ...? viy nyeh vazraJa-yetyeh,
yeslee ya ...? [вы не возражаете, если я ...?]
never mind nyeh vaJna [не важно]
mine: it's mine eta ma-yo [это моё]
mineral water meenyeralna-ya vada
[минеральная вода]
minimum meeneemoom [минимум]
minus meenoos [минус]
minute meenoota [минута]
in a minute cheryez meenootoo [через
минуту]
just a minute meenootachkoo [минуточку]
mirror zyerkala [зеркало]
miss: I miss you ya byez tebya skoocha-yoo [я
без тебя скучаю]
he's missing on prapal [он пропал]
there is a ... missing zdyes nyet ... [здесь
нет ...]
Miss see **Mr**
mist tooman [туман]
mistake asheepka [ошибка]
I think you've made a mistake mnyeh
kaJetsa, zdyes asheepka [мне кажется, здесь
ошибка]
misunderstanding nyeda-razoomyenee-yeh
[недоразумение]
modern savryemyeni [современный]
Monday panyedyelneek [понедельник]
money dyengee [деньги]
I've lost my money (men/women)
ya patyeryal/patyeryala dyengee
[я потерял/потеряла деньги]
month myesyats [месяц]
one month adeen myesyats [один месяц]
moon loona [луна]
more bolsheh [больше]
can I have some more? moJna yesho? [можно
ещё?]

more beer, please yesho peeva, paJalsta [ещё пиво, пожалуйста]

no more, thanks fsyo, spaseeba [всё, спасибо]

more comfortable oodobnyeh-yeh [удобнее]

more than ... bolsheh chem ... [больше чем ...]

morning ootra [утро]

good morning dobra-yeh ootra [доброе утро]

in the morning ootrum [утром]

this morning syevodnya ootram [сегодня утром]

Moscow Maskva [Москва]

mosquito kamar [комар]

most: I like it the most mnyeh eta bolsheh fsyevo nraveetsa [мне это больше всего нравится]

most of the time/the people bolsha-ya chast vryemyenee/lyoodyay [большая часть времени/людей]

motel matyel [мотель]

mother mat [мать]

motor mator [мотор]

motorbike matatseekl [мотоцикл]

motorboat matorna-ya lotka [моторная лодка]

motorcyclist matatseekleest [мотоциклист]

motorist avtamabeeleest [автомобилист]

motorway avtastrada [автострада]

mountain gara [гора]

mouse miysh [мышь]

moustache oosiy [усы]

mouth rot [рот]

move: don't move nyeh dveegItyes [не двигайтесь]

could you move your car? viy nyeh maglee biy choot-choot atyeHat? [вы не могли бы чуть-чуть отъехать?]

Mr/Mrs/Ms

>> *TRAVEL TIP: no equivalent for English titles; see* **first name**

much mnoga [много]

much better namnoga loochsheh [намного лучше]

much more namnoga bolsheh [намного больше]

not much nyemnoga [немного]

mug: I've been mugged na menya napalee [на меня напали]

mum mama [мама]

muscle miyshtsa [мышца]

museum moozyay [музей]

mushroom greep [гриб]

music moozika [музыка]

must: I must have ... mnyeh nooJna ... [мне нужно ...]

I must not eat ... mnyeh nyelzya yest ... [мне нельзя есть ...]

you must ... vam nooJna ... [вам нужно ...]

must I ...? mnyeh nooJna ...? [мне нужно ...?]

mustard garcheetsa [горчица]

my: my room *(in hotel)* moy nomyer [мой номер]

my hotel maya gasteeneetsa [моя гостиница]

nail *(finger)* nogat [ноготь]

(in wood) gvozd [гвоздь]

nail clippers sheepcheekee dlya nagtyay [щипчики для ногтей]

nail file peelka dlya nagtyay [пилка для ногтей]

nail polish lak dlya nagtyay [лак для ногтей]

nail scissors maneekyoorni-yeh noJneetsi [маникюрные ножницы]

naked goli [голый]

name eemya [имя]

my name is ... menya zavoot ... [меня зовут ...]

what's your name? kak vas zavoot? [как вас зовут?]

>> *TRAVEL TIP: Russians introduce themselves by their full name (e.g. Petrov, Boris Ivanovich) or they omit the patronymic (Petrov, Boris); surnames usually precede the first name*

napkin salfyetka [салфетка]

nappy pyelyonka [пелёнка]

narrow oozkee [узкий]

....

national natsee-onalni [национальный]

nationality natsee-onalnast [национальность]

natural natooralni [натуральный]

naughty: don't be naughty nyeh kapreezneechI [не капризничай]

near: is it near? eta ryadam? [это рядом?]

  near here zdyes ryadam [здесь рядом]

  do you go near ...? viy pra-yedyetyeh meema ...? [вы проедете мимо ...?]

  where's the nearest ...? gdyeh bleeJIshee ...? [где ближайший ...?]

nearly pachtee [почти]

neat: a neat whisky prosta veeskee [просто виски]

necessary nyeh-abHadeemi [необходимый]

  it's not necessary nyeh nada [не надо]

neck sheh-ya [шея]

necklace aJeryehlyeh [ожерелье]

need: I need a ... mnyeh nada ... [мне надо ...]

needle eegolka [иголка]

neighbour sasyed [сосед]

neither: I want neither ... nor ... ya nyeh Hachoo nee ... nee ... [я не хочу ни ... ни ...]

  neither do I ya toJeh [я тоже]

nephew plyemyaneek [племянник]

nervous nyervni [нервный]

never neekagda [никогда]

  well I never! nada Jeh! [надо же!]

new novi [новый]

  New Year Novi god [Новый год]

  New Year's Eve navagodnya-ya noch [новогодняя ночь]

  Happy New Year! sNovim godam! [с Новым годом!]

» *TRAVEL TIP: New Year is a favourite holiday for the Russians; they exchange gifts and have all-night parties; January 1 is a public holiday*

news novastee [новости]

newsagent's *(kiosk)* gazyetni kee-osk [газетный киоск]

newspaper gazyeta [газета]

  do you have any English newspapers? oo

vas yest angleeskee-yeh gazyeti? [у вас есть английские газеты?]

New Zealand Nova-ya Zyelandee-ya [Новая Зеландия]

(adj) nava-zyelandskee [новозеландский]

next slyedoo-yooshee [следующий]

please stop at the next corner paJalsta, astanaveetyeh na oogloo [пожалуйста, остановите на углу]

see you next year ooveedeemsa v boodooshem gadoo [увидимся в будущем году]

next week na slyedoo-yooshay nyedyelyeh [на следующей неделе]

next Tuesday fslyedoo-yooshee ftorneek [в следующий вторник]

sit next to me syad ryadam samnoy [сядь рядом со мной]

nice pree-yatni [приятный]

(food, drink) fkoosni [вкусный]

niece plyemyaneetsa [племянница]

night noch [ночь]

good night spakoynoy nochee [спокойной ночи]

at night nochoo [ночью]

nightclub nachnoy kloob [ночной клуб]

night-life nachna-ya Jeezn [ночная жизнь]

night porter nachnoy partyeh [ночной портье]

no nyet [нет]

there's no water nyet vadiy [нет воды]

I've no money oo menya nyet dyenyeg [у меня нет денег]

no way! nee-za-shto! [ни за что!]

nobody neekto [никто]

nobody saw it neekto nyeh veedyel [никто не видел]

noisy shoomni [шумный]

our room is too noisy v nashem nomyeryeh ochen shoomna [в нашем номере очень шумно]

none: none of them (people) neekto eez neeH [никто из них]

(things) neekakoy eez neeH [никакой из них]

....

nonsense yeroond*a* [ерунда]
normal narm*a*lni [нормальный]
north s*y*evyer [север]
Northern Ireland S*y*evyerna-ya Eerlandee-ya
 [Северная Ирландия]
nose nos [нос]
nosebleed nasav*o*-yeh kravatyech*e*nee-yeh
 [носовое кровотечение]
not nyeh [не]
 not that one nyeh tot [не тот]
 not me/you nyeh ya/tiy [не я/ты]
 not here/there nyeh zdyes/tam [не
 здесь/там]
 I'm not hungry (*men/women*) ya nyeh
 goladyen/galadn*a* [я не голоден/голодна]
 I don't want to … ya nyeh H*a*choo … [я не
 хочу …]
 he didn't tell me on mnyeh nyeh skaz*a*l [он
 мне не сказал]
 » *TRAVEL TIP: avoid negative questions; to the*
 question 'didn't you go?' a Russian could
 answer either 'yes' or 'no' and both might mean
 'no'
nothing neech*e*vo [ничего]
 there's nothing left neech*e*vo nyeh ast*a*las
 [ничего не осталось]
 nothing for me thanks mnyeh neech*e*vo nyeh
 noo*J*na, spas*ee*ba [мне ничего не нужно,
 спасибо]
November na-*y*abr [ноябрь]
now syaych*a*s [сейчас]
nowhere neegd*ye*h [нигде]
 there's nowhere to sit n*y*egdyeh syest [негде
 сесть]
nuisance: it's a nuisance nyepree-*ya*tna
 [неприятно]
 this man's being a nuisance *e*tat chelav*y*ek
 preest*a*-*yot* kamn*ye*h [этот человек пристаёт
 ко мне]
numb: my leg has gone numb (*men/women*)
 ya atseed*y*el/atseed*y*ela nogoo
 [я отсидел/отсидела ногу]

number *(figure)* cheeslo [число]
  (room, telephone etc) nomyer [номер]
number plate namyernoy znak [номерной знак]
nurse myedsyestra [медсестра]
nut *(for eating)* aryeH [орех]
  (for bolt) gIka [гайка]
oar vyeslo [весло]
obligatory abyazatyelni [обязательный]
obviously acheveedna [очевидно]
occasionally eenagda [иногда]
occupied *(toilet)* zanyata [занято]
  is this seat occupied? zdyes zanyata? [здесь занято?]
o'clock: 3 o'clock tree chasa [три часа]
October aktyabr [октябрь]
odd *(number)* nyechotni [нечётный]
  (strange) strani [странный]
of: the name of the hotel nazvanee-yeh gasteeneetsi [название гостиницы]
off: the milk/meat is off malako/myasa eesporteelas [молоко/мясо испортилось]
  it just came off on prosta slamalsa [он просто сломался]
  10% off skeedka dyesyat pratsentaf [скидка десять процентов]
offence narooshenee-yeh [нарушение]
office: the director's office kabeenyet deeryektara [кабинет директора]
  he works in an office on rabota-yet vofeesyeh [он работает в офисе]
officer *(to policeman)* tavareesh meeleetsee-anyer [товарищ милиционер]
official *(noun)* slooJashee [служащий]
often chasta [часто]
  not often nyechasta [нечасто]
oil masla [масло]
  will you change the oil? pamyenyItyeh masla, paJalsta [поменяйте масло, пожалуйста]
ointment maz [мазь]
OK ladna [ладно]
old stari [старый]

....

how old are you? sk*o*lka vam lyet? [сколько вам лет?]

YOU MAY WANT TO SAY ...

I am 25 mnyeh dv*a*dsat pyat lyet [мне двадцать пять лет]

omelette aml*y*et [омлет]

on na [на]

  on the table na stal*yeh* [на столе]

  I haven't got it on me oo men*ya* nyet *e*tava s sab*oy* [у меня нет этого с собой]

  on Friday fpy*a*tneetsoo [в пятницу]

  on television pa tyelyev*ee*zaroo [по телевизору]

once ad*ee*n raz [один раз]

  at once sr*a*zoo Jeh [сразу же]

one ad*ee*n [один]

  the red one kr*a*sni [красный]

onion look [лук]

only t*o*lka [только]

open *(not closed)* atkr*i*yti [открытый]

  I can't open it ya nyeh mag*oo e*ta atkr*i*yt [я не могу это открыть]

  when do you open? kagd*a* viy atkriv*a*-yetyeh? [когда вы открываете?]

opera *o*pyera [опера]

operation apyer*a*tsee-ya [операция]

  will I need an operation? mnyeh noo**J**na apyer*a*tsee-ya? [мне нужна операция?]

operator tyelyefan*ee*stka [телефонистка]

opposite: opposite the hotel naprot*ee*f gast*ee*neetsi [напротив гостиницы]

optician opt*ee*ka [оптика]

or *ee*lee [или]

orange *(fruit)* apyels*ee*n [апельсин]

  (colour) aran**J**evi [оранжевый]

orange juice apyels*ee*navi sok [апельсиновый сок]

order: could we order now? mo**J**na zakaz*a*t syaych*a*s? [можно заказать сейчас?]

  thank you, we've already ordered miy oo**J**eh zakazal*ee* [мы уже заказали]

  (noun: in commerce) zakaz [заказ]

Orthodox pravaslavni [православный]
other: the other one droogoy [другой]
  do you have any others? oo vas yest droogee-yeh? [у вас есть другие?]
otherwise eenacheh [иначе]
ought: I ought to go mnyeh nooJna eedtee [мне нужно идти]
ounce oontsee-ya [унция]
 )) *TRAVEL TIP: 1 ounce = 28.35 grammes*
our: our hotel nasha gasteeneetsa [наша гостиница]
  that's ours eta nasheh [это наше]
out: we're out of petrol oo nas koncheelsa byenzeen [у нас кончился бензин]
  get out! ooHadeetyeh! [уходите!]
outdoors na atkriytam vozdooHyeh [на открытом воздухе]
outside: I'd like a table outside ya Hachoo stoleek na ooleetsyeh [я хочу столик на улице]
over: over here vot zdyes [вот здесь]
  over there von tam [вон там]
  over ... *(more than)* bolsheh chem ... [больше чем ...]
  it's all over fsyo koncheelas [всё кончилось]
overboard: man overboard! chelavyek za bartom! [человек за бортом!]
overcharge: you've overcharged me viy smenya sleeshkam mnoga vzyalee [вы с меня слишком много взяли]
 )) *TRAVEL TIP: it's not uncommon for there to be a mistake in a bill; to be on the safe side, check all your bills, especially in restaurants*
overcooked pyeryevaryeni [переваренный]
overexposed *(photo)* pyeryedyerJani [передержанный]
overnight *(travel etc)* nachnoy [ночной]
oversleep prospat [проспать]
  I overslept *(men/women)* ya praspal/praspala [я проспал/проспала]
overtake abganyat [обгонять]
owe: what do I owe you? *(men/women)* skolka

....

ya vam dolJen/dalJna? [сколько я вам
должен/должна?]

own: my own ... moy sobstvyeni ... [мой
собственный ...]

are you on your own? *(to a man/woman)* viy
adeen/adna? [вы один/одна?]

I'm on my own *(men/women)* ya adeen/adna [я
один/одна]

owner vladyelyets [владелец]

oxygen keeslarod [кислород]

oyster oostreetsa [устрица]

pack: I haven't packed yet *(men/women)* ya
yesho nyeh sabral/sabrala vyeshee [я ещё не
собрал/собрала вещи]

can I have a packed lunch? moJna
paloocheet abyed sooHeem pIkom? [можно
получить обед сухим пайком?]

package tour tooreesteecheska-ya pa-yezdka
[туристическая поездка]

page *(of book)* straneetsa [страница]

pain bol [боль]

I've got a pain in my chest oo menya bolee
vgroodee [у меня боли в груди]

painkillers balyeh-ootalya-yoosheh-yeh
[болеутоляющее]

painting Jeevapees [живопись]

Pakistan Pakeestan [Пакистан]

Pakistani *(adj)* pakeestanskee [пакистанский]

pale blyedni [бледный]

pancake bleeniy [блины]

panties trooseekee [трусики]

pants bryookee [брюки]

(underpants) troosiy [трусы]

paper boomaga [бумага]

(newspaper) gazyeta [газета]

paracetamol paratsetamol [парацетамол]

parcel pasiylka [посылка]

pardon? *(didn't understand)* prasteetyeh?
[простите?]

I beg your pardon *(sorry)* eezveeneetyeh,
paJalsta [извините, пожалуйста]

parents radeetyelee [родители]

park *(noun)* park [парк]
  where can I park my car? gdyeh moJna
  pastaveet masheenoo? [где можно поставить
  машину?]
part chast [часть]
partner *(boyfriend/girlfriend)* droog/padrooga
  [друг/подруга]
  (business) partnyor [партнёр]
party *(political)* partee-ya [партия]
  (celebration) vyechereenka [вечеринка]
  I'm with the ... party ya eez ... groopi [я из ...
  группы]
  party member chlen partee [член партии]
pass *(mountain)* pyeryeval [перевал]
  he's passed out on patyeryal saznanee-yeh
  [он потерял сознание]
passable: is this road passable? pa etay
  darogyeh moJna yeHat? [по этой дороге
  можно ехать?]
passenger pasaJeer [пассажир]
passer-by praHoJee [прохожий]
passport paspart [паспорт]
past: in the past fproshlam [в прошлом]
pastry *(cake)* peeroJna-yeh [пирожное]
path trapeenka [тропинка]
patient: be patient boodtyeh tyerpyeleevi
  [будьте терпеливы]
patronymic otchestva [отчество]; *see*
  first name
pattern oozor [узор]
pavement tratoo-ar [тротуар]
pay plateet [платить]
  can I pay, please? moJna zaplateet? [можно
  заплатить?]
peace *(calm)* pakoy [покой]
  (not war) meer [мир]
peach pyerseek [персик]
peanuts araHees [арахис]
pear groosha [груша]
pearl Jemchoog [жемчуг]
peas garoH [горох]
pedal *(noun)* pyedal [педаль]

....

pedestrian pyesheHot [пешеход]
pedestrian crossing pyesheHodni pyeryeHot
  [пешеходный переход]
» *TRAVEL TIP: as drivers do not give way to*
  pedestrians as much as in the UK, always look
  for a pedestrian crossing
peg *(for washing)* preeshepka [прищепка]
pelvis taz [таз]
pen roochka [ручка]
  have you got a pen? oo vas yest roochka? [у
  вас есть ручка?]
pencil karandash [карандаш]
penfriend *(male/female)* droog/padrooga pa
  pyeryepeeskyeh [друг/подруга по переписке]
penicillin pyeneetseeleen [пенициллин]
penknife pyeracheeni noJeek [перочинный
  ножик]
pensioner pyensee-onyer [пенсионер]
people lyoodee [люди]
  the Russian people rooskee-yeh [русские]
pepper pyerets [перец]
peppermint myatna-ya kanfyeta [мятная
  конфета]
per: per night/per week/per person
  fsootkee/vnyedyelyoo/za chelavyeka [в сутки/в
  неделю/за человека]
per cent pratsent [процент]
perfect eede-alni [идеальный]
  the perfect holiday eede-alni otpoosk
  [идеальный отпуск]
perfume dooHee [духи]
perhaps moJet biyt [может быть]
period *(of time)* pyeree-ad [период]
  (menstruation) myenstroo-atsee-ya
  [менструация]
perm Heemeecheska-ya zaveevka [химическая
  завивка]
permit *(noun)* razryeshenee-yeh [разрешение]
person chelavyek [человек]
  in person leechna [лично]
personal stereo player [плейер]
petrol byenzeen [бензин]

petrol station byenzakalonka [бензоколонка]
»» *TRAVEL TIP: Russian-made cars run on A-79
and A-93 petrol and foreign cars on A-95 petrol;
lead-free petrol is not readily available*
phonecard
»» *TRAVEL TIP: all payphones are coin-operated*
photograph fatagrafee-ya [фотография]
  would you take a photograph of us?
  sfatagrafeerootyeh nas, paJalsta
  [сфотографируйте нас, пожалуйста]
piano pee-aneena [пианино]
pickpocket vor-karmaneek [вор-карманник]
picture karteena [картина]
pie peerog [пирог]
piece koosok [кусок]
  a piece of ... koosok ... [кусок ...]
pig sveenya [свинья]
pigeon goloop [голубь]
pile-up *(noun)* tsepna-ya avaree-ya [цепная
авария]
pill tablyetka [таблетка]
  (contraceptives) prateeva-zachatachni-yeh
  tablyetkee [противозачаточные таблетки]; *see*
  contraceptive
pillow padooshka [подушка]
pin boolafka [булавка]
pine sasna [сосна]
pineapple ananas [ананас]
pint
»» *TRAVEL TIP: 1 pint = 0.57 litres; see* **beer**
pipe *(for smoking)* troopka [трубка]
  (for water etc) troobapravot [трубопровод]
pipe tobacco troobachni tabak [трубочный
табак]
pity: it's a pity Jal [жаль]
place myesta [место]
  is this place taken? eta myesta zanyata? [это
  место занято?]
  do you know any good places to go? kooda
  zdyes sto-eet pItee? [куда здесь стоит пойти?]
plain *(not patterned)* adnatoni [однотонный]
  (food) prastoy [простой]

plane samalyot [самолёт]
  by plane samalyotam [самолётом]
plant *(flower etc)* rastyenee-yeh [растение]
plaster *(cast)* geeps [гипс]
  (sticking) plastiyr [пластырь]
plastic plastmasavi [пластмассовый]
plastic bag plasteekavi pakyet [пластиковый
  пакет]
plate taryelka [тарелка]
platform *(station)* platforma [платформа]
  which platform please? skaJeetyeh, paJalsta,
  kaka-ya platforma? [скажите, пожалуйста,
  какая платформа?]
play *(verb)* eegrat [играть]
  (theatre) pyesa [пьеса]
pleasant pree-yatni [приятный]
please: could you please ...? nyeh maglee biy
  viy ...? [не могли бы вы ...?]
  (yes) please da, spaseeba [да, спасибо]
pleasure oodavolstvee-yeh [удовольствие]
  it's a pleasure ochen pree-yatna [очень
  приятно]
plenty: plenty of ... mnoga ... [много ...]
  thank you, that's plenty spaseeba,
  dastatachna [спасибо, достаточно]
pliers plaskagooptsi [плоскогубцы]
plug *(electrical)* veelka [вилка]
  (sink) propka [пробка]
» *TRAVEL TIP: see* **electricity**
plum sleeva [слива]
plumber santyeHneek [сантехник]
plus plyoos [плюс]
pneumonia vaspalyenee-yeh lyoHkeeH
  [воспаление лёгких]
pocket karman [карман]
point: could you point to it? pakaJeetyeh, shto
  eta? [покажите, что это?]
  two point five dvyeh tseliH pyat dyesyatiH
  [две целых пять десятых]
points *(car)* kantakt [контакт]
Poland Polsha [Польша]
police paleetsee-ya [полиция]

get the police viyzaveeteyeh meeleetsee-yoo [вызовите милицию]

» *TRAVEL TIP: in emergencies, dial 02 (in Moscow) free of charge from a public phone*

policeman meeleetsee-anyer [милиционер]

police station atdyelyenee-yeh meeleetsee [отделение милиции]

polish *(noun: for shoes)* kryem dlya oboovee [крем для обуви]

　will you polish my shoes? moJetyeh pacheesteet ma-ee tooflee? [можете почистить мои туфли?]

polite vyeJleevi [вежливый]

politics paleeteeka [политика]

polluted zagryaznyoni [загрязнённый]

pool *(swimming)* basyayn [бассейн]

poor byedni [бедный]

　poor quality neezka-yeh kachestva [низкое качество]

popular papoolyarni [популярный]

population nasyelyenee-yeh [население]

pork sveeneena [свинина]

port *(harbour)* port [порт]
　(drink) partvyayn [портвейн]

porter *(in hotel)* shvyaytsar [швейцар]
　(at station etc) naseelsheek [носильщик]

portrait partryet [портрет]

posh *(hotel etc)* sheekarni [шикарный]

possible vazmoJni [возможный]

　could you possibly ...? nyeh maglee biy viy ...? [не могли бы вы ...?]

post *(noun: mail)* pochta [почта]

postcard atkriytka [открытка]

poste restante da vastryebavanee-ya [до востребования]

post office pochta [почта]

» *TRAVEL TIP: postboxes are red or blue; blue ones are for overseas and out of town mail; the central post office in Moscow is open until 9 p.m.; sending mail from a hotel is more reliable*

potato kartofyel [картофель]

pottery kyerameeka [керамика]

....

pound *(money)* foont styerleengav [фунт
стерлингов]
   (weight) foont [фунт]
» *TRAVEL TIP: conversion:* $\frac{pounds}{11} \times 5 = kilos$

pounds	1	3	5	6	7	8	9
kilos	0.45	1.4	2.3	2.7	3.2	3.6	4.1

pour: it's pouring doJd lyot [дождь льёт]
powder *(for face)* poodra [пудра]
power cut atklyoochenee-yeh elyektreechestva
   [отключение электричества]
power point razyetka [розетка]
prawns kryevyetkee [креветки]
prefer: I prefer this one ya pryedpacheeta-yoo
   eta [я предпочитаю это]
pregnant byeryemyena-ya [беременная]
prescription ryetsept [рецепт]
present: at present tyepyer [теперь]
   here's a present for you etat padarak dlya
   vas [этот подарок для вас]
president *(of country)* pryezeedyent [президент]
   (of firm) pryedsyedatyel [председатель]
press: could you press these? pagladtyeh,
   paJalsta [погладьте, пожалуйста]
pretty seempateechni [симпатичный]
   pretty good nyeploHa [неплохо]
price tsena [цена]
priest svyasheneek [священник]
printed matter pechatni matyeree-al
   [печатный материал]
prison tyoorma [тюрьма]
private chastni [частный]
probably vyera-yatna [вероятно]
problem prablyema [проблема]
product pradookt [продукт]
profit preebil [прибыль]
promise: do you promise? viy abyesha-yetyeh?
   [вы обещаете?]
   I promise ya abyesha-yoo [я обещаю]
pronounce pra-eeznyestee [произнести]
   how do you pronounce this? kak
   pra-eeznyestee eta? [как произнести это?]

....

properly praveelna [правильно]
property sobstvyenast [собственность]
prostitute prasteetootka [проститутка]
protect zasheeshat [защищать]
Protestant pratyestantskee [протестантский]
proud gordi [гордый]
prove: I can prove it ya magoo eta dakazat [я могу это доказать]
public: the public poobleeka [публика]
public bath banya [баня]
public holiday fsyenarodni prazdneek [всенародный праздник]

» *TRAVEL TIP: public holidays in Russia are:*
1 January Novi god [Новый год] *New Year*
7 January RaJdyestvo [Рождество] *Orthodox Christmas*
8 March Jenskee dyen [Женский день] *Women's Day*
1 and 2 May Pyerva-ya maya [Первое мая] *Labour Day*
9 May Dyen pabyedi [День победы] *Victory Day*
12 June Dyen nezaveeseemastee [День независимости] *Independence Day*
7 and 8 November Syedmo-yeh na-yabrya [Седьмое ноября] *Revolution Day*
individual republics have their own holidays

public toilet too-alyet [туалет]
» *TRAVEL TIP: public toilets tend to be dirty; there are no vending machines; toilet paper is scarce so carry tissues; toilets in restaurants etc are cleaner and often have toilet paper*
pudding poodeenk [пудинг]
pull *(verb)* tyanoot [тянуть]
   he pulled out in front of me on viy-yeHal na darogoo pyeryeda-mnoy [он выехал на дорогу передо мной]
pump nasos [насос]
punctual: he's very punctual on ochen poonktoo-alni [он очень пунктуальный]
puncture prakol [прокол]
pure *(water, wool etc)* cheesti [чистый]

....

purple fee-al*y*etavi [фиолетовый]

purse kashel*y*ok [кошелёк]

push *(verb)* talk*a*t [толкать]

  don't push! nyeh talk*I*tyes! [не толкайтесь!]

pushchair d*y*etska-ya kal*y*aska [детская коляска]

put: where can I put ...? kood*a* mnyeh pala*J*eet ...? [куда мне положить ...?]

pyjamas pee*J*ama [пижама]

quality k*a*chestva [качество]

quarantine karant*ee*n [карантин]

quarter ch*e*tvyert [четверть]

a quarter of an hour chetvyert chas*a* [чертверть часа]

quay preech*a*l [причал]

question vapros [вопрос]

queue *(noun)* ocher*y*ed [очередь]

  (verb) sta-*y*at vocher*y*edee [стоять в очереди]

>> *TRAVEL TIP: an obligatory pastime for most Russians; in small shops, first find out the price of the goods, then pay at a till 'kasa' [касса] and take your receipt back to the goods counter*

quick b*i*ystri [быстрый]

quiet *tee*H*ee* [тихий]

  be quiet! *t*eesheh! [тише!]

quite *(fairly)* davolna [довольно]

  quite a lot davolna mnoga [довольно много]

radiator batar*y*a*y*a [батарея]

  (in car) radee-*a*ter [радиатор]

radio r*a*dee-o [радио]

rail: by rail po-*y*ezdam [поездом]

rain do*J*d [дождь]

  it's raining eed*y*ot do*J*d [идёт дождь]

raincoat plash [плащ]

rape *(noun)* eeznas*ee*lavanee-yeh [изнасилование]

rare r*y*edkee [редкий]

  (steak) skrov*y*oo [с кровью]

raspberry mal*ee*na [малина]

rat kr*i*ysa [крыса]

rather: I'd rather sit here ya l*o*ochsheh s*y*ad*o*o zdyes [я лучше сяду здесь]

I'd rather not go ya loochsheh nyeh pIdoo [я лучше не пойду]

it's rather hot davolna Jarka [довольно жарко]

raw siroy [сырой]

razor breetva [бритва]

razor blades lyezvee-yeh breetvi [лезвие бритвы]

read: you read it prachteetyeh eta [прочтите это]

something to read shto-neebood pacheetat [что-нибудь почитать]

ready: when will it be ready? kagda eta boodyet gatova? [когда это будет готово?]

I'm not ready yet *(men/women)* ya yesho nyeh gatof/gatova [я ещё не готов/готова]

real nasta-yashee [настоящий]

really dyaystveetyelna [действительно]

rear-view mirror zyerkala zadnyeva veeda [зеркало заднего вида]

reasonable *(price etc)* nyedaragoy [недорогой]

receipt kveetansee-ya [квитанция]

can I have a receipt please? d/tyeh kveetantsee-yoo, paJalsta [дайте квитанцию, пожалуйста]

recently nyedavna [недавно]

reception *(at hotel)* stoyka [стойка]

at reception oo stoykee [у стойки]

receptionist *(at hotel)* dyeJorni admeeneestrater [дежурный администратор]

recipe retsept [рецепт]

recommend: can you recommend ...? moJetyeh paryekamyendavat ...? [можете порекомендовать ...?]

record *(music)* plasteenka [пластинка]

red krasni [красный]

Red Square Krasna-ya ploshad [Красная площадь]

region oblast [область]

in this region vetay oblastee [в этой области]

....

registered letter zakazno-yeh peesmo [заказное письмо]

relax: I just want to relax ya prosta Hachoo raslabeetsa [я просто хочу расслабиться]
  relax! raslabtyes! [расслабьтесь!]

religion ryeleegee-ya [религия]

remember: don't you remember? viy nyeh pomneetyeh? [вы не помните?]
  I'll always remember ya nafsyegda zapomn-yoo [я навсегда запомню]
  something to remember you by shto-neebood na pamyat o tebyeh [что-нибудь на память о тебе]

rent: can I rent a car/bicycle? moJna vzyat naprakat masheenoo/vyelaseepyet? [можно взять напрокат машину/велосипед?]

repair: can you repair it? moJetyeh eta pacheeneet? [можете это починить?]

repeat: could you repeat that? pavtareetyeh, paJalsta [повторите, пожалуйста]

rescue (verb) spasat [спасать]

reservation pryedvareetyelni zakaz [предварительный заказ]
  I want to make a reservation for ... ya Hachoo sdyelat zakaz na ... [я хочу сделать заказ на ...]

reserve: can I reserve a seat for ...? moJna zakazat beelyet na ...? [можно заказать билет на ...?]

responsible atvyetsvyeni [ответственный]

rest: I've come here for a rest (men/women) ya pree-yeHal/pree-yeHala syooda atdiHat [я приехал/приехала сюда отдыхать]

restaurant ryestaran [ресторан]

retired na pyensee [на пенсии]

return ticket beelyet tooda ee abratna [билет туда и обратно]
  » TRAVEL TIP: only single tickets are for sale within the country; return tickets can be only be purchased abroad, usually as part of a package

reverse gear zadnee Hot [задний ход]

rheumatism ryevmateezm [ревматизм]

rib ryebr*o* [ребро]

rice rees [рис]

rich *(person)* bagat*i* [богатый]

   (food) peetat*y*elni [питательный]

ridiculous smyeshn*o*y [смешной]

right: that's right *e*ta prav*ee*lna [это правильно]

   you're right viy pr*a*vi [вы правы]

   on the right sprav*a* [справа]

   right now pr*y*ama syaych*a*s [прямо сейчас]

   right here pr*y*ama zdyes [прямо здесь]

ring *(on finger)* kaltso [кольцо]

   I'll ring you ya teb*y*eh pazvan*y*oo [я тебе позвоню]

ripe zr*y*eli [зрелый]

rip-off: it's a rip-off *e*ta abdeer*a*lovka [это обдираловка]

river ryek*a* [река]

road dar*o*ga [дорога]

   which is the road to …? gdyeh dar*o*ga na …? [где дорога на …?]

rob: I've been robbed men*y*a agr*a*beelee [меня ограбили]

rock skal*a* [скала]

   whisky on the rocks v*ee*skee sald*o*m [виски со льдом]

roll *(bread)* boolachka [булочка]

romantic raman*tee*cheskee [романтический]

roof kr*i*ysha [крыша]

room *(in hotel)* nomyer [номер]

   (in house) komnata [комната]

   have you got a single room/double room? oo vas yest adnam*y*estni nomyer/nomyer na dvo-*ee*H? [у вас есть одноместный номер/номер на двоих?]

   YOU MAY WANT TO SAY …

   for one night/for three nights na s*oo*tkee/na tr*o*-yeh sootak [на сутки/на трое суток]

   YOU MAY THEN HEAR …

   da, yest nomyer soodobstvamee *yes, we have one with a bathroom*

   svabodn*i*H myest nyet *we have no vacancies*

....

room service: do you have room service?
moJna zakazat yedoo vnomyer? [можно
заказать еду в номер?]
rope kanat [канат]
rose roza [роза]
rough *(person)* groobi [грубый]
  (sea) boorni [бурный]
roughly *(approximately)* preebleezeetyelna
[приблизительно]
round *(circular)* kroogli [круглый]
roundabout kroogavoy pavarot [круговой
поворот]
route marshroot [маршрут]
  which is the prettiest/fastest route?
  kaka-ya daroga sama-ya kraseeva-ya/
  karotka-ya? [какая дорога самая красивая/
  короткая?]
rowing boat lodka [лодка]
rubber *(material)* ryezeena [резина]
  (eraser) lasteek [ластик]
rubber band ryezeenka [резинка]
rubbish *(garbage)* mooser [мусор]
  (poor quality goods) baraHlo [барахло]
  rubbish! chepooHa! [чепуха!]
rucksack ryookzak [рюкзак]
rudder rool [руль]
rude groobi [грубый]
ruins razvaleeni [развалины]
rum rom [ром]
  rum and coke koka-kola sromam [кока-кола с
  ромом]
run: hurry, run! davI! byegom! [давай! бегом!]
  I've run out of petrol/money oo men-ya
  koncheelsa byenzeen/koncheelees dyengee [у
  меня кончился бензин/кончились деньги]
Russia Rassee-ya [Россия]
Russian *(adj, man)* rooskee [русский]
  (woman) rooska-ya [русская]
  (language) rooskee yaziyk [русский язык]
  the Russians rooskee-yeh [русские]
  I don't speak Russian ya nyeh gavaryoo
  pa-rooskee [я не говорю по-русски]

sad groostni [грустный]
safe *(not in danger)* vbyezapasnastee [в
  безопасности]
  will it be safe? eta nyeh apasna? [это не
  опасно?]
  is it safe to swim here? zdyes nyeh apasna
  plavat? [здесь не опасно плавать?]
safety pin angleeska-ya boolafka [английская
  булавка]
sail *(verb)* plavat (pod paroosam) [плавать (под
  парусом)]
sailboard syayl-bord [сейл-борд]
sailor maryak [моряк]
salad salat [салат]
salami salyamee [салями]
sale: is it for sale? eta prada-yotsa? [это
  продаётся?]
salmon lasos [лосось]
salt sol [соль]
same tot Jeh sami [тот же самый]
  the same again, please to Jeh sama-yeh,
  paJalsta [то же самое, пожалуйста]
  the same to you ee vam Jela-yoo tavo Jeh [и
  вам желаю того же!]
sand pyesok [песок]
sandals sandalee [сандали]
sandwich bootyerbrod [бутерброд]
sanitary towels geegee-yeneecheskee-yeh
  pakyeti [гигиенические пакеты]
satisfactory oodavlyetvareetyelni
  [удовлетворительный]
Saturday soobota [суббота]
sauce so-oos [соус]
saucepan kastryoolya [кастрюля]
saucer blyoodseh [блюдце]
sauna sa-oona [сауна]
sausage *(salami)* kalbasa [колбаса]
  (frankfurter) saseeska [сосиска]
say: how do you say ... in Russian? kak
  pa-rooskee ...? [как по-русски ...?]
  what did he say? shto on skazal? [что он
  сказал?]

....

scarf *(for neck)* sharf [шарф]
  (for head) platok [платок]
scenery pyayzaJ [пейзаж]
schedule grafeek [график]
  on schedule pa grafeekoo [по графику]
  behind schedule sapazdanee-yem [с опозданием]
  scheduled flight ryaysavi palyot [рейсовый полёт]
school shkola [школа]
scissors: a pair of scissors noJneetsi [ножницы]
scooter matarolyer [мотороллер]
Scotland Shotlandee-ya [Шотландия]
Scottish shotlandskee [шотландский]
scratch *(noun)* tsarapeena [царапина]
scream *(verb)* kreechat [кричать]
screw *(noun)* vint [винт]
screwdriver atvyortka [отвёртка]
sea moryeh [море]
  by the sea oo morya [у моря]
seafood marskee-yeh pradookti [морские продукты]
search *(verb)* eeskat [искать]
search party po-eeskovi atryad [поисковый отряд]
seasick: I get seasick menya ookacheeva-yet [меня укачивает]
seaside: at the seaside na byeryegoo morya [на берегу моря]
  let's go to the seaside davItyeh pa-yedyem kmoryoo [давайте поедем к морю]
season vryemya goda [время года]
seasoning preeprava [приправа]
seat myesta [место]
  is this somebody's seat? eta myesta zanyata? [это место занято?]
seat belt ryemyen [ремень]
second *(adj)* ftaroy [второй]
  (time) syekoonda [секунда]
  just a second syekoondachkoo [секундочку]
secondhand padyerJani [подержанный]

see v*ee*dyet [видеть]
  oh, I see pan*ya*tna [понятно]
  have you seen ...? viy nyeh v*ee*dyelee...? [вы не видели ...?]
  can I see the room? moJna pasmatr*y*et nomyer? [можно посмотреть номер?]
seem: it seems so paH*o*Jeh, shto tak [похоже, что так]
seldom *ee*zryedka [изредка]
  it seldom works ry*e*dka rabota-yet [редко работает]
self-service sama-absl*oo*Jeevanee-yeh [самообслуживание]
sell pradav*a*t [продавать]
send pasil*a*t [посылать]
sentimental syentyement*a*lni [сентиментальный]
separate *(adj)* atdy*e*lni [отдельный]
  I'm separated *(men/women)* ya nyeh Jeev*oo* s Jen*o*y/mooJem [я не живу с женой/мужем]
  can we pay separately? moJna zaplat*ee*t pa atdy*e*lnastee? [можно заплатить по отдельности?]
September syent*ya*br [сентябрь]
serious syery*o*zni [серёзный]
  I'm serious ya gavary*oo* syery*o*zna [я говорю серьёзно]
  this is serious *e*ta syery*o*zna [это серьёзно]
  is it serious, doctor? *e*ta ap*a*sna, d*o*kter? [это опасно, доктор?]
service: the service was excellent/poor absl*oo*Jeevalee pryekr*a*sna/pl*o*Ha [обслуживали прекрасно/плохо]
service station *(for repairs)* stantsee-ya tyeHabsl*oo*Jeevanee-ya [станция техобслуживания]
serviette salf*y*etka [салфетка]
several ny*e*skolka [несколько]
sexy preevlyek*a*tyelni [привлекательный]
shade: in the shade vty*e*n*ee* [в тени]
shake: to shake hands paJ*a*t rook*oo* [пожать руку]

....

shallow myelkee [мелкий]
shame: what a shame! kak Jal! [как жаль!]
shampoo shampoon [шампунь]
share: to share a room/table biyt vmyestyeh v komnatyeh/za stalom [быть вместе в комнате/за столом]
sharp ostri [острый]
shave: to have a shave breetsa [бриться]
shaver breetva [бритва]
shaving foam pyena dlya breetya [пена для бритья]
shaving point razyetka dlya elyektrabreetv [розетка для электробритв]
shawl shal [шаль]
she ana [она]
sheep aftsa [овца]
sheet *(linen)* prastinya [простыня]
shelf polka [полка]
shell rakooshka [ракушка]
shellfish malyoosk [моллюск]
shelter pree-yoot [приют]
   can we shelter here? moJna zdyes pyeryeJdat? [можно здесь переждать?]
sherry Heres [херес]
ship karabl [корабль]
shirt roobashka [рубашка]
shock *(noun)* shok [шок]
   I got an electric shock menya oodareela tokam [меня ударило током]
shock-absorber amorteezater [амортизатор]
shoes oboov [обувь]
shop magazeen [магазин]
   I've some shopping to do mnyeh nooJna ko-yeh-shto koopeet [мне нужно кое-что купить]
shore byeryeg [берег]
short *(person)* nyevisokee [невысокий]
   (holiday) karotkee [короткий]
   I'm three short tryoH nyeHvata-yet [трёх не хватает]
short cut: is there a short cut? moJna pra-yeHat napryamoo-yoo? [можно проехать

напрямую?]

shorts shorti [шорты]

shoulder plyech*o* [плечо]

shout kreech*a*t [кричать]

show: please show me paka*J*eetyeh, pa*J*alsta [покажите, пожалуйста]

shower: with shower sd*oo*shem [с душем]

shrimps kryevyetkee [креветки]

shut: it was shut b*i*yla zakr*i*yta [было закрыто]

   when do you shut? kagd*a* zakriv*a*-yetyeh? [когда закрываете?]

   shut up! zamalch*ee!* [замолчи!]

shy zastyencheevi [застенчивый]

sick *(ill)* baln*o*y [больной]

   I feel sick men*ya* tashn*ee*t [меня тошнит]

   he's been sick yev*o* stashn*ee*la [его стошнило]

side starana [сторона]

   by the side of the road na abocheenyeh [на обочине]

side lights padf*a*rneekee [подфарники]

side street pyeryeh-*oo*lak [переулок]

sight: it's out of sight yev*o* nyeh v*ee*dna [его не видно]

sightseeing tour eksk*oo*rsee-ya [экскурсия]

   we'd like to go on a sightseeing tour miy biy Hat*y*elee pa-*ye*Hat na eksk*oo*rsee-y*oo* [мы бы хотели поехать на экскурсию]

sign *(notice)* znak [знак]

signal: he didn't signal *(driver)* on nyeh seegn*a*leel [он не сигналил]

signature podpees [подпись]

silence teesheen*a* [тишина]

silk sholk [шёлк]

silly gl*oo*pi [глупый]

silver syeryebro [серебро]

similar padobni [подобный]

simple prast*o*y [простой]

since *(because)* tak kak [так как]

   since last week sproshlay nyed*y*elee [с прошлой недели]

....

since we arrived *(from that time)* styeH por, kak miy pree-*ye*Halee [с тех пор, как мы приехали]

sincere *ee*skryeni [искренный]

　yours sincerely *ee*skryenyeh vash [искренне ваш]

sing pyet [петь]

single ad*ee*n [один]

　single room adnamyestni nomyer [одноместный номер]

　I'm single *(men/women)* ya nyeh Jenat/zamooJem [я не женат/замужем]

　a single to ... beelyet do ... [билет до ...]

sink: it sank on ootonool [он утонул]

sister syestr*a* [сестра]

sit: can I sit here? moJna zdyes syest? [можно здесь сесть?]

size razmyer [размер]

ski *(verb)* katatsa na liyJaH [кататься на лыжах]

　skis liyJee [лыжи]

ski boots liyJni-yeh bateenkee [лыжные ботинки]

ski lift padyomneek [подъёмник]

ski pass *(for ski lift)* kartachka-propoosk [карточка-пропуск]

ski poles liyJni-yeh palkee [лыжные палки]

skid *(verb)* zanaseet [заносить]

skin koJa [кожа]

skirt *yoo*pka [юбка]

sky nyeba [небо]

sleep: I can't sleep ya nyeh magoo zasnoot [я не могу заснуть]

　YOU MAY HEAR ...

　Harasho spalee? *did you sleep well?*

sleeper *(rail)* spalni vagon [спальный вагон]

sleeping bag spalni myeshok [спальный мешок]

sleeping pills snatvorni-yeh tablyetkee [снотворные таблетки]

sleeve rookaf [рукав]

slide *(photo)* slId [слайд]

slippers tapachkee [тапочки]
slow myedlyeni [медленный]
  could you speak a little slower? gavareetyeh
  myedlyenyeh-yeh, paJalsta [говорите
  медленнее, пожалуйста]
small malyenkee [маленький]
  small change myelach [мелочь]
smell: there's a funny smell zdyes kakoy-ta
  strani zapaH [здесь какой-то странный
  запах]
  it smells ploHa paHnyet [плохо пахнет]
smile (verb) oolibatsa [улыбаться]
smoke (noun) diym [дым]
  do you smoke? viy kooreetyeh? [вы курите?]
  can I smoke? moJna kooreet? [можно
  курить?]
  I don't smoke ya nyeh kooryoo [я не курю]
smooth gladkee [гладкий]
snack: can we just have a snack? moJna
  prosta pyeryekooseet? [можно просто
  перекусить?]
snow snyeg [снег]
  it's snowing snyeg eedyot [снег идёт]
snowstorm myetyel [метель]
so: it's so hot today syevodnya ochen Jarka
  [сегодня очень жарко]
  not so much nyeh tak mnoga [не так много]
  so-so tak syebyeh [так себе]
soaking solution (for contact lenses) rastvor
  dlya leenz [раствор для линз]
soap miyla [мыло]
soap powder steeralni parashok [стиральный
  порошок]
sober tryezvi [трезвый]
sock nasok [носок]
soda (water) gazeerovana-ya vada
  [газированная вода]
soft drink byezalkagolni napeetak
  [безалкогольный напиток]
soldier saldat [солдат]
sole (of foot) stoopnya [ступня]
  (of shoe) padoshva [подошва]

some: some people nyekatori-yeh lyoodee [некоторые люди]

can I have some? dItyeh mnyeh, paJalsta [дайте мне, пожалуйста]

can I have some grapes/some bread? dItyeh mnyeh, paJalsta, veenagrad/Hlyeb [дайте мне, пожалуйста, виноград/хлеб]

can I have some more? yesho, paJalsta [ещё, пожалуйста]

that's some drink! *(delicious, strong)* noo ee napeetak! [ну и напиток!]

somebody kto-neebood [кто-нибудь]

something shto-neebood [что-нибудь]

sometime kagda-neebood [когда-нибудь]

sometimes eenagda [иногда]

somewhere gdyeh-neebood [где-нибудь]

son siyn [сын]

song pyesnya [песня]

soon skora [скоро]

as soon as possible kak moJna skaryeh-yeh [как можно скорее]

sooner skaryeh-yeh [скорее]

sore: it's sore baleet [болит]

I have a sore throat oo menya baleet gorla [у меня болит горло]

sorry: (I'm) sorry prashoo prashenee-ya [прошу прощения]

» *TRAVEL TIP: apologies are used with people you know, but the rules don't always apply to strangers; don't expect an apology if someone bumps into you on the street!*

sort: this sort takoy [такой]

what sort of ...? kakoy ...? [какой ...?]

will you sort it out? razbyereetyes, paJalsta [разберитесь, пожалуйста]

soup soop [суп]

sour keesli [кислый]

south yook [юг]

South Africa YooJna-ya Afreeka [Южная Африка]

South African *(adj)* yooJna-afreekanskee [южно-африканский]

souvenir soovyen*eer* [сувенир]

Soviet sav*y*etskee [советский]

Soviet Union Sav*y*etskee Sa-*yooz* [Советский Союз]

spade lap*a*ta [лопата]

spanner g*a*-yechni kly*ooch* [гаечный ключ]

spare: spare part zapch*a*st [запчасть]

   spare wheel zapasno-yeh kalyes*o* [запасное колесо]

spark(ing) plug svyech*a* zaJeegan*ee*-ya [свеча зажигания]

speak: do you speak English? viy gavar*ee*tyeh pa-angl*ee*skee? [вы говорите по-английски?]

   I don't speak ... ya nyeh gavar*yoo* pa-... [я не говорю по-...]

special spetsee-*a*lni [специальный]

specialist spetsee-al*ee*st [специалист]

specially spetsee-*a*lna [специально]

spectacles achk*ee* [очки]

speed sk*o*rast [скорость]

   he was speeding on pryev*iy*seel sk*o*rast [он превысил скорость]

speed limit makseem*a*lna-ya sk*o*rast [максимальная скорость]

» *TRAVEL TIP: maximum speed limits are low due to poor road conditions; on motorways, the limit is 90 kph and in built-up areas it's 50 kph*

speedometer speedomyetr [спидометр]

spend *(money)* trat*ee*t [тратить]

spice pry*a*nast [пряность]

   is it spicy? eta pry*a*na-yeh bly*oo*da? [это пряное блюдо?]

spider pa-*ook* [паук]

spirits *(drink)* alkag*o*l [алкоголь]

spoon lo*J*ka [ложка]

sprain: I've sprained my ... *(men/women)* ya rastyan*oo*l/rastyan*oo*la ... [я растянул/растянула ...]

spring *(in seat etc)* ryes*o*ra [рессора]

   (season) vyesn*a* [весна]

square *(in town)* pl*o*shad [площадь]

   2 square metres dva kvadr*a*tniH my*e*tra [два

....

квадратных метра]

stairs lyesneetsa [лестница]

stale *(food)* nyesvyeJee [несвежий]

stalls parter [партер]

stamp marka [марка]

  two stamps for overseas dvyeh myeJdoonarodni-yeh markee, paJalsta [две международные марки, пожалуйста]

standard *(adj)* standartni [стандартный]

star zvyezda [звезда]

start *(noun)* nachala [начало]

  (verb) nacheenat [начинать]

  my car won't start ma-ya masheena nyeh zavodeetsa [моя машина не заводится]

  when does it start? kagda nachala? [когда начало?]

starter *(food)* zakooska [закуска]

starving: I'm starving *(men/women)* ya goladyen/galadna [я голоден/голодна]

state *(country)* gasoodarstva [государство]

  (adj) gasoodarstvyeni [государственный]

station *(main, rail)* vakzal [вокзал]

  (underground) stantsee-ya [станция]

statue statoo-ya [статуя]

stay: we enjoyed our stay nam zdyes ochen panraveelas [нам здесь очень понравилось]

  stay there astantyes tam [останьтесь там]

  I'm staying at Hotel ... *(men/women)* ya astanaveelsa/astanaveelas v gasteeneetsyeh ... [я остановился/остановилась в гостинице ...]

steak beefshtyeks [бифштекс]

  YOU MAY HEAR ...

  kak paJareet beefshtyeks? *how would you like your steak?*

  skrovyoo? *rare?*

  sryednyeh? *medium?*

  Harasho praJareet? *well done?*

steep krootoy [крутой]

steering wheel rool [руль]

step *(noun)* stoopyenka [ступенька]

stereo styereh-o [стерео]

....

sterling *(money)* foont styerleengaf [фунт стерлингов]

stewardess styoo-ardyesa [стюардесса]

sticking plaster plastir [пластырь]

sticky leepkee [липкий]

stiff Jostkee [жёсткий]

still: keep still! nyeh dveegItyes! [не двигайтесь!]

  I'm still here ya yesho zdyes [я ещё здесь]

stink *(noun)* von [вонь]

stolen: my wallet's been stolen oo menya ookralee boomaJneek [у меня украли бумажник]

stomach Jeloodak [желудок]

  I have stomach-ache oo menya baleet Jeloodak [у меня болит желудок]

  have you got something for an upset stomach? oo vas yest shto-neebood at rastroystva Jeloodka? [у вас есть что-нибудь от расстройства желудка?]

stone kamyen [камень]

» *TRAVEL TIP: 1 stone = 6.35 kilos*

stop: do you stop near ...? viy astanavleeva-yetyes oo ...? [вы останавливаетесь у ...?]

  stop! astanaveetyes! [остановитесь!]

stop-over: can we make a stop-over in St Petersburg? moJna sdyelat astanovkoo v Sankt Pyetyerboorgyeh? [можно сделать остановку в Санкт Петербурге?]

  (overnight) nachofka [ночёвка]

storm boorya [буря]

St Petersburg Sankt Pyetyerboorg [Санкт Петербург]

straight pryamoy [прямой]

  go straight on eedeetyeh pryama [идите прямо]

  straight away nyemyedlyena [немедленно]

  straight whisky cheesta-yeh veeskee [чистое виски]

strange *(odd)* strani [странный]

  (unknown) nyeznakomi [незнакомый]

....

stranger *(man/woman)*
nyeznakomyets/nyeznakomka
[незнакомец/незнакомка]
  I'm a stranger here *(men/women)* ya zdyes
  chooJoy/chooJa-ya [я здесь чужой/чужая]
strawberry kloobneeka [клубника]
street ooleetsa [улица]
string vyeryofka [верёвка]
stroke: he's had a stroke oo nyevo biyl oodar
  [у него был удар]
strong *(person, material)* seelni [сильный]
  (drink) kryepkee [крепкий]
student *(man/woman)* stoodyent/stoodyentka
  [студент/студентка]
stung: I've been stung by a wasp menya
  ookooseela asa [меня укусила оса]
stupid gloopi [глупый]
such: such a lot tak mnoga [так много]
suddenly vdroog [вдруг]
sugar saHar [сахар]
suit *(man's, woman's)* kastyoom [костюм]
suitable padHadyashee [походящий]
suitcase chemadan [чемодан]
summer lyeta [лето]
sun sontseh [солнце]
  in the sun na sontseh [на солнце]
  out of the sun vtyenee [в тени]
sunbathe zagarat [загорать]
sunblock sryedstva proteef zagara [средство
  против загара]
sunburn solnyechni aJok [солнечный ожог]
Sunday vaskryesyenyeh [воскресенье]
  » *TRAVEL TIP: banks and government offices are
  closed on Sundays and so are most shops;
  markets and hard currency shops are open*
sunglasses tyomni-yeh achkee [тёмные очки]
sunstroke solnyechni oodar [солнечный удар]
suntan lotion lasyon at zagara [лосьон от
  загара]
  » *TRAVEL TIP: you won't find suntan lotion in the
  shops so take a supply with you*
supermarket soopyermarkyet [супермаркет]

supper ooJeen [ужин]

sure: I'm not sure (men/women) ya nyeh oovyeryen/oovyeryena [я не уверен/уверена]

are you sure? viy oovyeryeni? [вы уверены?]

sure! kanyeshna! [конечно!]

surname fameelee-ya [фамилия]

» *TRAVEL TIP: when addressing someone or asking for someone on the phone, it is polite to use their first name and patronymic; see also* **first name**

swearword roogatyelstva [ругательство]

sweat (verb) patyet [потеть]

sweet (dessert) dyesyert [десерт]

sweets kanfyeti [конфеты]

it's too sweet sleeshkam slatka-yeh [слишком сладкое]

swerve: I had to swerve (men/women) ya dolJen biyl/dalJna biyla ryezka svyernoot [я должен был/должна была резко свернуть]

swim: I'm going for a swim pIdoo paplava-yoo [пойду поплаваю]

let's go for a swim pashlee paplava-yem [пошли поплаваем]

swimming costume koopalneek [купальник]

swimming trunks plafkee [плавки]

switch (noun) viyklyoochatyel [выключатель]

to switch on/off vkloocheet/viykloocheet [включить/выключить]

table stol [стол]

a table for four stoleek na chetvyeriH [столик на четверых]

take brat [брать]

can I take this (with me)? moJna eta vzyat? [можно это взять?]

will you take me to the airport? moJetyeh atvyeztee menya veraport? [можете отвезти меня в аэропорт?]

how long will it take? skolka vryemyenee eta zImyot? [сколько времени это займёт?]

somebody has taken my bags kto-to vzyal ma-ee soomkee [кто-то взял мои сумки]

can I take you out tonight? miy moJem

∙∙

fstryeteetsa syevodnya vyecheram? [мы
можем встретиться сегодня вечером?]

talcum powder talk [тальк]

talk *(verb)* razgavareevat [разговаривать]

tall visokee [высокий]

tampons tamponi [тампоны]

》 *TRAVEL TIP: take your own supplies with you;
not available from vending machines*

tan *(noun)* zagar [загар]

I want to get a tan ya Hachoo zagaryet [я
хочу загореть]

tank *(of car)* bak [бак]

tap kran [кран]

tape *(cassette)* magneetafona-ya kasyeta
[магнитофонная кассета]

(sticky) klyayka-ya lyenta [клейкая лента]

tape recorder magneetafon [магнитофон]

tariff *(list of charges)* tareef [тариф]

taste *(noun)* fkoos [вкус]

can I taste it? moJna paprobavat? [можно
попробовать?]

it tastes horrible gadast [гадость]

it tastes very nice eta ochen fkoosna [это
очень вкусно]

taxi taksee [такси]

will you get me a taxi? nIdeetyeh mnyeh,
paJalsta, taksee [найдите мне, пожалуйста,
такси]

where can I get a taxi? gdyeh moJna pImat
taksee? [где можно поймать такси?]

》 *TRAVEL TIP: although taxis are metered, drivers
sometimes refuse to take you unless you pay in
hard currency or give a huge tip; beware of taxi
drivers approaching you at the airport – their
prices can be exorbitant*

taxi driver vadeetyel taksee [водитель такси]

tea chI [чай]

could I have a cup of tea? chashkoo cha-yoo,
paJalsta [чашку чаю, пожалуйста]

with milk/with lemon smalakom/sleemonam
[с молоком/с лимоном]

》 *TRAVEL TIP: Russian tea is hardly ever served*

with milk, except with hotel breakfasts

teach: could you teach me ...? viy maglee biy
menya na-oocheet ...? [вы могли бы меня
научить ...?]

teacher *(man/woman)*
oocheetyel/oocheetyelneetsa
[учитель/учительница]

telegram tyelyegrama [телеграмма]

I want to send a telegram ya Hachoo paslat
tyelyegramoo [я хочу послать телеграмму]

telephone *(noun)* tyelyefon [телефон]
YOU MAY WANT TO SAY ...

can I make a phone call? moJna pazvaneet?
[можно позвонить?]

can I speak to Olga? Olgoo papraseetyeh,
paJalsta [Ольгу попросите, пожалуйста]

could you get number ... for me? mnyeh
nooJen nomyer ... [мне нужен номер ...]

» *TRAVEL TIP: public phones are easy to find but
are all operated with coins; few are reliable
enough for inter-city calls and none for
international calls; it's best to phone from your
hotel and book international calls through the
operator or use the post office*

telephone directory tyelyefoni spravachneek
[телефонный справочник]

television *(set)* tyelyeveezer [телевизор]
(medium) tyelyeveedyenee-yeh [телевидение]

I'd like to watch television ya Hachoo
smatryet tyelyeveezer [я хочу смотреть
телевизор]

tell: could you tell me where ...? skaJeetyeh
mnyeh, paJalsta, gdyeh ...? [скажите мне,
пожалуйста, где ...?]

temperature tyempyeratoora [температура]

he's got a temperature oo nyevo
tyempyeratoora [у него температура]

tennis tyenees [теннис]

tennis ball tyeneesni myach [теннисный мяч]

tennis court tyeneesni kort [теннисный корт]

tennis racket tyeneesna-ya rakyetka
[теннисная ракетка]

....

tent palatka [палатка]
terminus *(rail, underground)* kanyechna-ya
  stantsee-ya [конечная станция]
  (bus, tram) kanyechna-ya astanofka [конечная
  остановка]
terrible ooJasni [ужасный]
terrific zamyechatyelni [замечательный]
than chem [чем]
  bigger than ... bolsheh chem ... [больше
  чем ...]
thanks/thank you spaseeba [спасибо]
  no thank you nyet, spaseeba [нет, спасибо]
  thank you very much balsho-yeh spaseeba
  [большое спасибо]
  thank you for your help spaseeba za pomash
  [спасибо за помощь]
  YOU MAY THEN HEAR ...
  paJalsta! *you're welcome!*
  nyeh-za-shto! *it's nothing!*
that *(pronoun)* eta [это]
  (adj) tot [тот]
  that man/that woman tot mooJcheena/ta
  Jensheena [тот мужчина/та женщина]
  I would like that one ya Hachoo vot tot [я
  хочу вот тот]
  how do you say that? kak eta skazat? [как
  это сказать?]
  I think that ... dooma-yoo, shto ... [думаю,
  что ...]
thaw *(noun)* otyepyel [оттепель]
the *Russian has no word for 'the'*
theatre teh-atr [театр]
their eeH [их]
  it's their bag eta eeH soomka [это их сумка]
  it's theirs eta eeH [это их]
them: I haven't seen them *(men/women)* ya
  eeH nyeh veedyel/veedyela [я их не
  видел/видела]
  with them sneemee [с ними]
  who - them? kto - anee? [кто – они?]
then *(at that time)* fto vryemya [в то время]
  (after that) patom [потом]

there tam [там]
   how do I get there? kak tooda dabratsa? [как туда добраться?]
   is there/are there ...?
   eemyeh-yetsa/eemyeh-yootsa lee ...?
   [имеется/имеются ли ...?]
   there is/there are ...
   eemyeh-yetsa/eemyeh-yootsa ...
   [имеется/имеются ...]
   there you are (*offering*) eta vam [это вам]
thermal spring garyachee eestochneek
   [горячий источник]
these (*pronoun*) etee [эти]
   can I take these? moJna vzyat vot etee?
   [можно взять вот эти?]
they anee [они]
   they are friends of mine anee ma-ee droozya
   [они мои друзья]
thick (*wood*) goostoy [густой]
thief vor [вор]
thigh byedro [бедро]
thin (*body*) Hoodoy [худой]
thing vyesh [вещь]
   I've lost all my things (*men/women*) ya
   patyeryal/patyeryala fsyeh vyeshee [я
   потерял/потеряла все вещи]
think doomat [думать]
   I'll think it over ya padooma-yoo [я подумаю]
   I think so dooma-yoo shto da [думаю что да]
   I don't think so ya tak nyeh dooma-yoo [я так
   не думаю]
third (*adj*) tryetee [третий]
thirsty: I'm thirsty mnyeh Hochetsa peet [мне
   хочется пить]
this (*pronoun*) etat [этот]
   this hotel/this house/this letter eta
   gasteeneetsa/etat dom/eta peesmo [эта
   гостиница/этот дом/это письмо]
   can I have this one? moJna vot eta? [можно
   вот это?]
   this is my wife eta ma-ya Jena [это моя жена]
   is this ...? eta ...? [это ...?]

....

this is ... eta ... [это ...]
those *(pronoun)* tyeh [те]
  no, not these, those! nyeh etee, a vot tyeh!
  [не эти, а вот те!]
thread *(noun)* neetka [нитка]
throat gorla [горло]
throttle *(motorbike)* drosyel [дроссель]
through: through Minsk cheryez Meensk
  [через Минск]
throw *(verb)* brasat [бросать]
thumb balshoy palyets [большой палец]
thunder *(noun)* grom [гром]
thunderstorm graza [гроза]
Thursday chetvyerk [четверг]
ticket beelyet [билет]
tie *(necktie)* galstook [галстук]
tight *(clothes)* oozkee [узкий]
tights kalgotkee [колготки]
time vryemya [время]
  what's the time? katori chas? [который час?]
  I haven't got time oo menya nyet vryemyenee
  [у меня нет времени]
  for the time being paka [пока]
  this time vetat raz [в этот раз]
  last time fproshli raz [в прошлый раз]
  next time fslyedoo-yooshee raz [в следующий
  раз]
  3 times tree raza [три раза]
  have a good time! fsyevo Harosheva! [всего
  хорошего!]
» *TRAVEL TIP: how to tell the time: key words are*
  [минута] 'meenoota' *(minute),* [час] 'chas' *(hour),*
  [половина] 'palaveena' *(half)*
  it's one o'clock chas [час]
  it's two/three o'clock dva/tree chasa
  [два/три часа]
  it's four/five/six o'clock chetiyreh/pyat/shest
  chasof [четыре/пять/шесть часов]
  it's 5/10/20/25 past seven
  pyat/dyesat/dvatsat/dvatsat pyat meenoot
  vasmova [пять/десять/двадцать/двадцать
  пять минут восьмого]

it's quarter past eight/eight fifteen
chetvyert dyevyatava [четверть девятого]
it's half past nine/nine thirty palaveena
dyesyatava [половина десятого]
it's 25/20/10/5 to ten byez dvatsatee
pyatee/dvatsatee/dyesyatee/pyatee dyesat [без
двадцати пяти/двадцати/десяти/пяти
десять]
it's quarter to eleven/10.45 byez chetvyertee
adeenatsat [без четверти одиннадцать]
at twelve o'clock at night/in the afternoon
vdvyenatsat chasof nochee/dnya [в
двенадцать часов ночи/дня]
timetable raspeesanee-yeh [расписание]
tin *(can)* kansyervna-ya banka [консервная
банка]
tin-opener kansyervni noJ [консервный нож]
tip *(noun)* cha-yeviy-yeh [чаевые]
» *TRAVEL TIP: tipping is widespread and at times
borders on bribing; gaining entry to popular
bars and restaurants is sometimes helped by
'tipping' the doorman*
tired oostali [усталый]
I'm tired *(men/women)* ya oostal/oostala [я
устал/устала]
tissues boomaJni-yeh nasaviy-yeh platkee
[бумажные носовые платки]
to: to Moscow v Maskvoo [в Москву]
toast tost [тост]
tobacco tabak [табак]
tobacconist's tabachni kee-osk [табачный
киоск]
today syevodnya [сегодня]
toe palyets nagee [палец ноги]
together vmyestyeh [вместе]
we're together miy vmyestyeh [мы вместе]
can we pay all together? moJna zaplateet za
fsyo vmyestyeh? [можно заплатить за всё
вместе?]
toilet too-alyet [туалет]
where are the toilets? gdyeh too-alyet? [где
туалет?]

....

I have to go to the toilet mnyeh nooJna vtoo-al*y*et [мне нужно в туалет]

there's no toilet paper nyet too-al*y*etnay boom*a*gee [нет туалетной бумаги]; *see* **public toilet**

tomato pameed*or* [помидор]

tomato juice tam*a*tni sok [томатный сок]

tomato ketchup k*y*etch*oo*p [кетчуп]

tomorrow z*a*ftra [завтра]

tomorrow morning/afternoon/evening z*a*ftra *oo*tram/dnyom/v*y*echeram [завтра утром/днём/вечером]

the day after tomorrow paslyez*a*ftra [послезавтра]

see you tomorrow da z*a*ftra [до завтра]

ton t*o*na [тонна]

» *TRAVEL TIP: 1 ton = 1.016 kilos*

tongue yaz*i*yk [язык]

tonic (water) t*o*neek [тоник]

tonight syev*o*dnya v*y*echeram [сегодня вечером]

tonne t*o*na [тонна]

» *TRAVEL TIP: 1 tonne = 1.000 kilos = metric ton*

tonsillitis tanzeel*ee*t [тонзиллит]

too *(also)* toJeh [тоже]

that's too much *e*ta sl*ee*shkam mn*o*ga [это слишком много]

(too expensive) sl*ee*shkam d*o*raga [слишком дорого]

not too fast, please nyeh tak b*i*ystra, paJ*a*lsta [не так быстро, пожалуйста]

tool eenstroom*y*ent [инструмент]

tooth zoop [зуб]

I've got toothache oo men*ya* bal*ee*t zoop [у меня болит зуб]

toothbrush zoobn*a*-ya sh*o*tka [зубная щётка]

toothpaste zoobn*a*-ya p*a*sta [зубная паста]

top: on top of ... na ... [на ...]

on the top floor na vyerHnyem etaJeh [на верхнем этаже]

at the top navyerH*oo* [наверху]

total *(noun)* eet*o*k [итог]

tough *(meat)* Jostkee [жёсткий]

tour *(noun)* ekskoorsee-ya [экскурсия]

   we'd like to go on a tour of the town miy Hateem pa-yeHat na ekskoorsee-yoo pa goradoo [мы хотим поехать на экскурсию по городу]

   we're touring around miy pootyeshestvoo-yem [мы путешествуем]

tour guide ekskoorsavod [экскурсовод]

tourist tooreest [турист]

   I'm a tourist *(men/women)* ya tooreest/tooreestka [я турист/туристка]

tourist office tooreesteecheska-yeh byooro [туристическое бюро]

tow *(verb)* vyeztee na bookseeryeh [везти на буксире]

   can you give me a tow? moJetyeh vzyat na bookseer? [можете взять на буксир?]

towards k [к]

   he was coming straight towards me on yeHal pryama na menya [он ехал прямо на меня]

towel palatyentseh [полотенце]

town gorat [город]

   in town vgoradyeh [в городе]

   would you take me into the town? viy moJetyeh atvyeztee menya v gorat? [вы можете отвезти меня в город?]

towrope kanat [канат]

traditional tradeetsee-oni [традиционный]

   a traditional Russian meal tradeetsee-ona-yeh rooska-yeh yeda [традиционная русская еда]

traffic dveeJenee-yeh [движение]

traffic lights svyetafor [светофор]

traffic police 'ga-ee' [ГАИ]

train po-yezd [поезд]

» *TRAVEL TIP: trains are quite dirty and not very punctual; now with rising inflation, costs are unpredictable; you might find that, as a tourist, you can only pay for a ticket with hard currency; but although officially illegal, it's common for people to ask a Russian friend to buy their ticket for them with roubles which will be cheaper*

trainers krasofkee [кроссовки]

tram tramv*I* [трамвай]

tranquillizers trankveeleezatari [транквилизаторы]

translate pyeryevad*ee*t [переводить]
 would you translate that for me?
 pyeryeh-vyed*ee*tyeh *e*ta, pa*J*alsta [переведите это, пожалуйста]

translator *(man/woman)*
 pyeryevodcheek/pyeryevodcheetsa [переводчик/переводчица]

transmission *(of car)* transmeesee-oni val [трансмиссионный вал]

Trans-Siberian Express trans-seeb*ee*rskee ekspres [транс-сибирский экспресс]

travel agent's byoor*o* pootyesh*e*stvee [бюро путешествий]

traveller's cheque daro*J*ni chek [дорожный чек]

» *TRAVEL TIP: the commission charge for changing traveller's cheques is much higher than for changing cash; in view of recent exchange rates, it's better to take low denomination notes with you; the situation is always changing – take advice from a travel agent before leaving*

tree dyeryeva [дерево]

tremendous agromni [огромный]

trim: just a trim, please t*o*lka nyemn*o*ga padravny*I*tyeh volasi, pa*J*alsta [только немного подровняйте волосы, пожалуйста]

trip *(noun)* pa-yezdka [поездка]
 we want to go on a trip to ... miy Hat*ee*m pa-ye*H*at v ... [мы хотим поехать в ...]

trouble *(noun)* nyepree-y*a*tnast [неприятность]
 I'm having trouble with ... oo men*y*a prablyemi s ... [у меня проблемы с ...]

trousers bryookee [брюки]

trout far*y*el [форель]

trolleybus troly*a*yboos [троллейбус]

true vyerna [верно]

it's not true eta nyepravda [это неправда]
try *(verb)* paprobavat [попробовать]
  please try paprobootyeh, paJalsta
  [попробуйте, пожалуйста]
  can I try it on? moJna pamyereet? [можно
  померить?]
tsar tsar [царь]
T-shirt footbolka [футболка]
Tuesday ftorneek [вторник]
turn: where do we turn off? gdyeh nam nada
  svyernoot? [где нам надо свернуть?]
  he turned without indicating on nyeh
  vklyoocheel seegnal na pavarotyeh [он не
  включил сигнал на повороте]
twice dvaJdi [дважды]
  twice as much vdva raza bolsheh [в два раза
  больше]
twin beds dvyeh adnaspalni-yeh kravatee [две
  односпальные кровати]
typewriter peeshoosha-ya masheenka
  [пишущая машинка]
typical teepeechni [типичный]
tyre sheena [шина]
  I need a new tyre mnyeh nooJna pamyenyat
  sheenoo [мне нужно поменять шину]

» *TRAVEL TIP: tyre pressure*

lb/sq in	18	20	22	24	26	28	30
kg/sq cm	1.3	1.4	1.5	1.7	1.8	2	2.1

ugly byezabrazni [безобразный]
ulcer yazva [язва]
Ulster Olstyer [Ольстер]
umbrella zonteek [зонтик]
uncle dyadya [дядя]
uncomfortable *(furniture etc)* nyeh-oodobni
  [неудобный]
unconscious byez saznanee-ya [без сознания]
under pod [под]
underdone: it's underdone nyeda-gatovlyen
  [недоготовлен]
underground *(rail)* myetro [метро]
understand: I understand ya paneema-yoo [я
  понимаю]

....

I don't understand ya nyeh paneema-yoo [я не понимаю]

do you understand? viy paneema-yet-yeh? [вы понимаете?]

undo (clothes etc) rastyogeevat [расстёгивать]

unfriendly nyedrooJelyoobni [недружелюбный]

unhappy nyeshastni [несчастный]

United States of America Sa-yedeenyoni-yeh Shtati Amyereekee [Соединённые Штаты Америки]

unlock atkrivat [открывать]

until do [до]

until next year do slyedoo-yoosheva goda [до следующего года]

unusual nyeh-abiknavyeni [необыкновенный]

up v-vyerH [вверх]

up there tam navyerHoo [там наверху]

it's up there eta von tam [это вон там]

he's not up yet (out of bed) on yesho nyeh fstal [он ещё не встал]

what's up? fchom dyela? [в чём дело?]

upside-down v-vyerH dnom [вверх дном]

upstairs navyerHoo [наверху]

urgent srochni [срочный]

us nas [нас]

he hasn't seen us on nas nyeh veedyel [он нас не видел]

use: can I use ...? moJna vaspolzavatsa ...? [можно воспользоваться ...?]

useful palyezni [полезный]

USSR 'es-es-es-er' [СССР]

usual abiknavyeni [обыкновенный]

as usual kak abiychna [как обычно]

usually abiychna [обычно]

U-turn razvarot [разворот]

vacancy: do you have any vacancies? (hotel) oo vas yest svabodni-yeh namyera? [у вас есть свободные номера?]

vacate (room) asvabadeet [освободить]

vaccination preeveevka [прививка]

vacuum flask tyermas [термос]

vagina vlagaleesheh [влагалище]
valid dyaystveetyelni [действительный]
  how long is it valid for? na skolka
  vryemyenee on dyaystveetyelyen? [на сколько
  времени он действителен?]
valuable tseni [ценный]
  will you look after my valuables? vam
  moJna atdat na Hranyenee-yeh dragatsenastee?
  [вам можно отдать на хранение
  драгоценности?]
value tsenast [ценность]
valve klapan [клапан]
van foorgon [фургон]
vanilla vaneel [ваниль]
varicose veins vareekozni-yeh vyeni
  [варикозные вены]
veal tyelyateena [телятина]
vegetables ovashee [овощи]
vegetarian *(man/woman)*
  vyegetaree-anyets/vyegetaree-anka
  [вегетарианец/вегетарианка]
ventilator vyenteelater [вентилятор]
very/very much ochen [очень]
via cheryez [через]
video camera veedeh-okamyera [видеокамера]
video cassette veedeh-okasyeta [видеокассета]
video shop veedeh-osalon [видеосалон]
village dyeryevnya [деревня]
vinegar ooksoos [уксус]
violent seelni [сильный]
visibility veedeemast [видимость]
visit *(verb)* pasyeshat [посещать]
vodka vodka [водка]
» *TRAVEL TIP: traditionally served neat in a small
  glass; swallow a piece of butter before you drink
  and eat something else immediately afterwards*
voice golas [голос]
voltage napryaJenee-yeh [напряжение]
» *TRAVEL TIP: voltage is 220*
waist talee-ya [талия]
wait: will we have to wait long? dolga Jdat?
  [долго ждать?]

....

wait for me padaJdeetyeh menya [подождите меня]

I'm waiting for a friend/my wife ya Jdoo drooga/Jenoo [я жду друга/жену]

waiter afeetsee-ant [официант]

waiter! afeetsee-ant! [официант!]

waitress afeesee-antka [официантка]

waitress! dyevooshka! [девушка!]

wake: will you wake me up at 7.30? paJalsta, razboodeetyeh menya vpalaveenyeh vasmova [пожалуйста, разбудите меня в половине восьмого]

Wales Oo-els [Уэльс]

walk: can we walk there? moJna dItee pyeshkom? [можно дойти пешком?]

are there any good walks around here? zdyes eentyeryesna Hadeet pyeshkom? [здесь интересно ходить пешком?]

walking shoes oboov dlya Hadbiy [обувь для ходьбы]

walking stick trost [трость]

wall styena [стена]

wallet boomaJneek [бумажник]

want: I want/she wants ... ya Hachoo/ana Hochet ... [я хочу/она хочет ...]

I want to talk to the consul ya Hachoo gavareet skonsoolam [я хочу говорить с консулом]

what do you want? shto viy Hateetyeh? [что вы хотите?]

I don't want to ya nyeh Hachoo [я не хочу]

warm tyopli [тёплый]

warning pryedoo-pryeJdyenee-yeh [предупреждение]

was: I was ... *(men/women)* ya biyl/biyla ... [я был/была ...]

he was ... on biyl ... [он был ...]

it was ... eta biyla ... [это было ...]

wash: can you wash these for me? moJetyeh pasteerat eta dlya menya? [можете постирать это для меня?]

where can I wash? gdyeh moJna pamiytsa?

....

[где можно помыться?]

washer *(for nut)* prakladka [прокладка]

washing powder steeralni parashok
[стиральный порошок]

wasp asa [оса]

watch *(wrist-)* chasiy [часы]

  will you watch my bags for me?
preesmatreetyeh, paJalsta, za ma-yeemi
vyeshamee [присмотрите, пожалуйста, за
моими вещами]

  watch out! astaroJna! [осторожно!]

water vada [вода]

  can I have some water? dItyeh mnyeh
nyemnoga vadiy, paJalsta [дайте мне
немного воды, пожалуйста]

waterproof nyepramaka-yemi
[непромокаемый]

water-skiing vadnaliyJni sport [воднолыжный
спорт]

way: the Russian way pa rooskay tradeetsee
[по русский традиции]

  could you tell me the way to ...? kak papast
v ... [как попасть в ...]

  for answers see **where**

  no way! nee-za-shto! [ни за что!]

we miy [мы]

  we are British miy eez Veleekobreetanee [мы
из Великобритании]

weak slabi [слабый]

weather pagoda [погода]

  what filthy weather! kaka-ya
atvrateetyelna-ya pagoda! [какая
отвратительная погода!]

  what's the weather forecast? kakoy pragnoz
pagodi? [какой прогноз погоды?]

  YOU MAY THEN HEAR ...

  boodyet Jarka *it will be hot*

  vyera-yatna, boodyet doJd *it might rain*

Wednesday sryeda [среда]

week nyedyelya [неделя]

  a week today/tomorrow rovna cheryez
nyedyelyoo [ровно через неделю]

....

at the weekend v soobotoo-vaskryesyenyeh [в субботу-воскресенье]

weight vyes [вес]

well: I'm not feeling well ya sebya ploHa choostvoo-yoo [я себя плохо чувствую]

how are you? – very well, thanks kak dyela? – spaseeba, Harasho [как дела? – спасибо, хорошо]

you speak English very well viy ochen Harasho gavareetyeh pa-angleeskee [вы очень хорошо говорите по-английски]

wellingtons ryezeenavi-yeh sapagee [резиновые сапоги]

Welsh oo-elskee [уэльский]

were: you/we/they were ... viy/miy/anee biylee... [вы/мы/они были ...]

west zapat [запад]

the West Zapat [Запад]

West Indies Vest-eendee-ya [Вест-Индия]

wet mokri [мокрый]

what: what is that? shto-eta? [что это?]

what for? zachem? [зачем?]

what? (pardon?) shto? [что?]

wheel kalyeso [колесо]

when? kagda? [когда?]

when is breakfast? kagda zaftrak? [когда завтрак?]

where? gdyeh? [где?]

where is the post office? gdyeh pochta? [где почта?]

YOU MAY THEN HEAR ...

pryama *straight on*

pavyerneetyeh nalyeva *turn left*

pavyerneetyeh naprava *turn right*

ftaroy pavarot naprava/nalyeva *second on the right/left*

which: which bus? kakoy avtoboos? [какой автобус?]

which (one)? kakoy eez neeH? [какой из них?]

whisky veeskee [виски]

white byeli [белый]

who? kto? [кто?]

whose: whose is this? cho *eta*? [чьё это?]

why? pachem*oo*? [почему?]

   why not? pachem*oo* biy ee nyet? [почему бы и нет?]

   ok, why not? kak*a*-ya r*a*zneetsa! [какая разница!]

wide sheer*o*kee [широкий]

wife Jen*a* [жена]

will: when will it be finished? kagd*a* zakoncheetsa? [когда закончится?]

   will you do it? viy *eta* sdyela-yet-yeh? [вы это сделаете?]

   I will come back ya vyerno*os* [я вернусь]

wind *(noun)* vyetyer [ветер]

window akno [окно]

   near the window oo akn*a* [у окна]

windscreen vyetravo-yeh styeklo [ветровое стекло]

windscreen wipers styekla-acheest*ee*tyelee [стеклоочистители]

  » *TRAVEL TIP: always remove windscreen wipers when leaving the car; theft is common*

windsurfing veendsyerfeeng [виндсерфинг]

windy vyetryeni [ветреный]

wine veeno [вино]

   what kind of wine do you have? kak*ee*-yeh veen*a* oo vas yest? [какие вина у вас есть?]

  » *TRAVEL TIP: shortages are common; Georgian wines are the best but are not readily available*

winter zeem*a* [зима]

Winter Palace Z*ee*mnee dvaryets [Зимний дворец]

wire *(electrical)* provat [провод]

wish: best wishes sna-eelo*o*chsheemee paJel*a*nee-yamee [с наилучшими пожеланиями]

with s [с]

   with me samn*oy* [со мной]

without byez [без]

witness sveedyetyel [свидетель]

   will you act as a witness for me? moJetyeh biyt ma-*eem* sveedyetyel-yem? [можете быть

·····································

моим свидетелем?]

woman/women Jensheena/Jensheeni
[женщина/женщины]

wonderful zamyechatyelni [замечательный]

won't: it won't start nyeh zavodeetsa [не
заводится]

wood (*material*) dyeryeva [дерево]
(*forest*) lyes [лес]

wool sherst [шерсть]

word slova [слово]
   I don't know that word ya nyeh zna-yoo etava
   slova [я не знаю этого слова]

work (*verb*) rabotat [работать]
   (*noun*) rabota [работа]
   it's not working eta nyeh rabota-yet [это не
   работает]
   I work in London ya rabota-yoo v Londonyeh
   [я работаю в Лондоне]

worry (*noun*) tryevoga [тревога]
   don't worry nyeh byespakoytyes [не
   беспокойтесь]
   I'm worried about him ya byespako-yoos a
   nyom [я беспокоюсь о нём]

worse: it's worse eta Hoodeh [это хуже]
   he's getting worse yemoo Hoodeh [ему хуже]

worst sami plaHoy [самый плохой]

worth: it's not worth that much on etava
nyeh sto-eet [он этого не стоит]

worthwhile: is it worthwhile going? tooda
sto-yeet pa-yeHat? [туда стоит поехать?]

wrap: could you wrap it up? zavyerneetyeh,
paJalsta [заверните, пожалуйста]

wrench (*tool*) ga-yechni klyooch [гаечный
ключ]

wrist zapyastyeh [запястье]

write peesat [писать]
   could you write it down? zapeesheetyeh,
   paJalsta [запишите, пожалуйста]
   I'll write to you ya boodoo peesat vam [я буду
   писать вам]

writing paper boomaga dlya peesma [бумага
для письма]

wrong nyepraveelna [неправильно]
  I think the bill's wrong ya dooma-yoo, shto shot nyetochni [я думаю, что счёт неточный]
  there's something wrong with … shto-ta nyeh tak s … [что-то не так с …]
  you're wrong viy nyepravi [вы неправы]
  sorry, wrong number *(men/women)* eezveeneetyeh, ya nyeh tooda papal/papala [я не туда попал/попала]

X-ray ryentgyenavskee sneemak [рентгеновский снимок]

yacht yaHta [яхта]

yard yard [ярд]
  » *TRAVEL TIP: 1 yard = 91.44 cms = 0.91 m*

year god [год]
  this year/next year vetam gadoo/na boodooshee god [в этом году/на будущий год]

yellow Jolti [жёлтый]

yes da [да]

yesterday fchera [вчера]
  the day before yesterday pazafchera [позавчера]
  yesterday morning/yesterday afternoon fchera ootram/fchera dnyom [вчера утром/вчера днём]

yet: is it ready yet? ooJeh gatova? [уже готово?]
  not yet yesho nyet [ещё нет]

yoghurt prastakvasha [простокваша]

you *(polite or plural)* viy [вы]
  (familiar and singular) tiy [ты]
  I like you viy mnyeh nraveetyes [вы мне нравитесь]
  with you svamee [с вами]
  » *TRAVEL TIP: we have generally given the formal and polite 'you' form in this book – 'viy' [вы] (it is also used when speaking to more than one person); with friends and young people (when speaking to one person), you should use the more familiar 'tiy' [ты]*

young maladoy [молодой]

••

your *(polite or plural)* vash [ваш]
  (familiar and singular) tvoy [твой]
  is this your camera? *e*ta vash foto-apar*a*t?
  [это ваш фотоаппарат?]
  is this yours? *e*ta v*a*sheh? [это ваше?]; *see* **you**
youth hostel malad*yo*Jna-ya gast*e*eneetsa
  [молодёжная гостиница]
zero nool [нуль]
  below zero n*ee*Jeh nool*y*a [ниже нуля]
zip molnee-ya [молния]

RUSSIAN SIGNS AND NOTICES

БИЛЕТЫ *tickets*
БОЛЬНИЦА *hospital*
ВХОД *entrance*
ВЫХОД *exit*
ДОРОЖНЫЕ РАБОТЫ *roadworks*
Ж *ladies' toilets*
ЖЕНСКИЙ ТУАЛЕТ *ladies' toilets*
ЗАКРЫТО *closed*
ЗАНЯТО *engaged*
ЗАЛ ОЖИДАНИЯ *waiting room*
ЗАПАСНОЙ ВЫХОД *emergency exit*
КАССА *cash desk*
ЛИФТ *lift*
М *gents; underground*
МЕСТО ДЛЯ КУРЕНИЯ *smoking area*
МИЛИЦИЯ *police*
МУЖСКОЙ ТУАЛЕТ *gents*
НА СЕБЯ *pull*
НЕ КУРИТЬ *no smoking*
НЕТ ВХОДА *no entry*
ОСТОРОЖНО *caution*
ОТКРЫТО *open*
ОТПРАВЛЕНИЕ *departures*
ОТ СЕБЯ *push*
РУКАМИ НЕ ТРОГАТЬ *don't touch*
ПОСТОРОННИМ ВХОД ВОСПРЕЩЁН *staff only*
ПРИБЫТИЕ *arrivals*
СВОБОДНО *vacant*
СВОБОДНЫХ МЕСТ НЕТ *no vacancies*
СЛУЖБА РАЗМЕЩЕНИЯ *reception desk*
СЛУЖЕБНЫЙ ВХОД *staff entrance*
СПРАВОЧНОЕ БЮРО *information desk*
СТАНЦИЯ ТЕХОБСЛУЖИВАНИЯ *service station*
СТОЛИК НЕ ОБСЛУЖИВАЕТСЯ *no service at this table*
ТАМОЖНЯ *Customs*
ТУАЛЕТ *toilet*
ЧАСЫ РАБОТЫ *opening hours*

....

0	nool	[нуль]
1	adeen	[один]
2	dva	[два]
3	tree	[три]
4	chetiyryeh	[четыре]
5	pyat	[пять]
6	shest	[шесть]
7	syem	[семь]
8	vosyem	[восемь]
9	dyevyat	[девять]
10	dyesyat	[десять]
11	adeenatsat	[одиннадцать]
12	dvyenatsat	[двенадцать]
13	treenatsat	[тринадцать]
14	chetiyrnatsat	[четырнадцать]
15	pyatnatsat	[пятнадцать]
16	shesnatsat	[шестнадцать]
17	syemnatsat	[семнадцать]
18	vasyemnatsat	[восемнадцать]
19	dyevyatnatsat	[девятнадцать]
20	dvatsat	[двадцать]
21	dvatsat adeen	[двадцать один]
22	dvatsat dva	[двадцать два]
30	treetsat	[тридцать]
31	treetsat adeen	[тридцать один]
40	sorak	[сорок]
50	pyadyesyat	[пятьдесят]
60	shesdyesyat	[шестьдесят]
70	syemdyesyat	[семьдесят]

80	vosyemdyesyat [восемьдесят]
90	dyevyanosta [девяносто]

100	sto [сто]
101	sto adeen [сто один]
200	dvyestee [двести]
300	treesta [триста]
1,000	tiysyacha [тысяча]
2,000	dvyeh tiysyachee [две тысячи]
3,000	tree tiysyachee [три тысячи]
4,655	chetiyryeh tiysyachee shestsot shestdyesyat pyat [четыре тысячи шестьсот шестдесят пять]

Dates: *to say the date in Russian use the ordinal number followed by the month:*

1st	pyerva-yeh [первое]
2nd	ftaro-yeh [второе]
3rd	tryetyeh [третье]
4th	chetvyorta-yeh [четвёртое]
5th	pyata-yeh [пятое]
6th	shesto-yeh [шестое]
7th	syedmo-yeh [седьмое]
8th	vasmo-yeh [восьмое]
9th	dyevyata-yeh [девятое]
10th	dyesyata-yeh [десятое]
14th	chetiyrnatsata-yeh [четырнадцатое]
15th	pyatnatsata-yeh [пятнадцатое]
20th	dvatsata-yeh [двадцатое]
21st	dvatsat pyerva-yeh [двадцать первое]
31st	treetsat pyerva-yeh [тридцать первое]

....

REPUBLICS, CITIES AND PLACES OF INTEREST

Азербайджан AzyerbIjan *Azerbaijan*
Армения Armyenee-ya *Armenia*
Белоруссия Byelaroosee-ya *Byelorussia*
Владивосток Vladeevastok *Vladivostok*
Волгоград Valgagrad *Volgograd*
Воронеж VaronyeJ *Voronezh*
Горький Gorkee *Gorky*
Грузия Groozee-ya *Georgia*
Загорск Zagorsk *Zagorsk*
Казахстан KazaHstan *Kazakhstan*
Кавказ Kafkaz *Caucasus*
Каспийское море Kaspeeska-yeh moryeh
   Caspian Sea
Киев Kee-yev *Kiev*
Киргизстан Keergeezstan *Kirgizstan*
Крым Kriym *Crimea*
Латвия Latvee-ya *Latvia*
Литва Leetva *Lithuania*
Минск Meensk Minsk
Молдова Maldova *Moldova*
Москва Maskva *Moscow*
Одесса Odyesa *Odessa*
Прибалтика Preebalteeka the Baltic States
Россия Rassee-ya *Russia*
Самарканд Samarkand *Samarkand*
Санкт Петербург Sankt Pyetyerboorg
   St Petersburg
Советский Союз
   Savyetskee Sa-yooz *Soviet Union*
Сочи Sochee *Sochi*
СССР 'es-es-es-er' *USSR*
Таджикистан Tadjeekeestan *Tadzhikistan*
Ташкент Tashkyent *Tashkent*
Тбилиси Tbeeleesee *Tbilisi*
Туркменистан Toorkmyeneestan
   Turkmenistan
Узбекистан Oozbyekeestan *Uzbekistan*
Укаина Ookra-eena *Ukraine*
Урал Ooral *Urals*
Чёрное море Chorna-yeh moryeh *Black Sea*
Эстония Estonee-ya *Estonia*
Ялта Yalta *Yalta*